10 HOUR SERIES

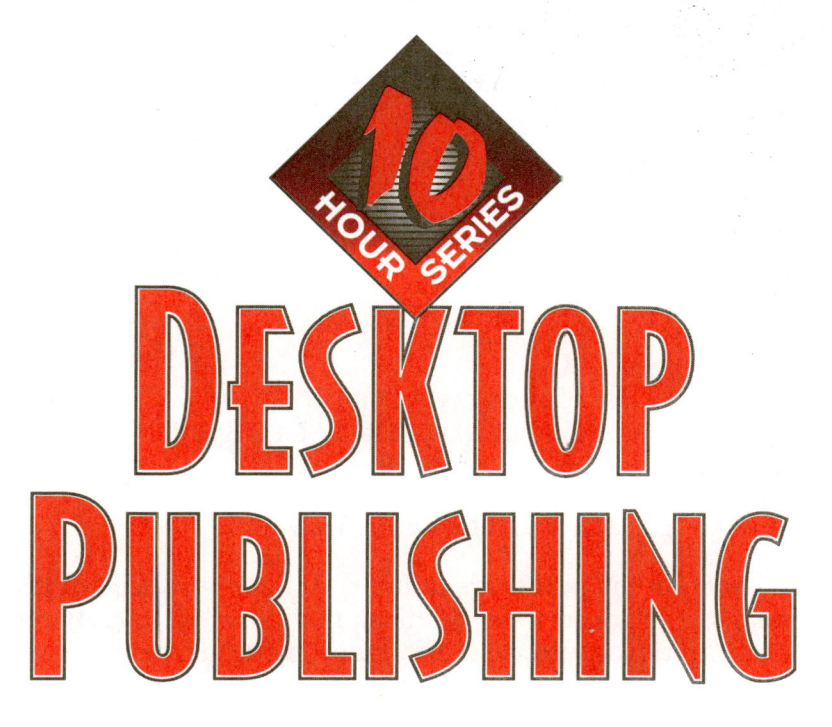

DESKTOP PUBLISHING

Susan E. L. Lake
Lubbock-Cooper High School
Lubbock, Texas

VISIT US ON THE INTERNET
www.swep.com

South-Western Educational Publishing
an International Thomson Publishing company I(T)P®
WWW: http://www.thomson.com

Cincinnati • Albany, NY • Belmont, CA • Bonn • Boston • Detroit • Johannesburg • London • Madrid
Melbourne • Mexico City • New York • Paris • Singapore • Tokyo • Toronto • Washington

Team Leader: Karen Schmohe
Project Manager: Jane Phelan
Editor: Kimberlee Kusnerak
Consulting Editor: Susan Bechtel
Production Coordinator: Jane Congdon
Manufacturing Coordinator: Carol Chase
Marketing Manager: Tim Gleim
Marketing Coordinator: Lisa Barto
Art/Design Coordinator: Darren Wright
Cover/Internal Design: Joe Pagliaro

Copyright © 2000
by SOUTH-WESTERN EDUCATIONAL PUBLISHING
Cincinnati, Ohio

ALL RIGHTS RESERVED

The text of this publication, or any part thereof, may not be reproduced or transmitted in any form or by any means, electronic or mechanical, including photocopying, recording, storage in an information retrieval system, or otherwise, without the prior written permission of the publisher.

I(T)P®
International Thomson Publishing

South-Western Educational Publishing is a division of International Thomson Publishing Inc. The ITP logo is a registered trademark used herein under license by South-Western Educational Publishing.

ISBN: 0-538-68754-1

1 2 3 4 5 6 7 WV 03 02 01 00 99
Printed in the United States of America

Microsoft® and Windows® are registered trademarks of Microsoft Corporation.

COREL® and WordPerfect® are registered trademarks of Corel Corporation or Corel Corporation Limited.

The names of commercially available software mentioned herein are used for identification purposes only and may be trademarks or registered trademarks of their respective owners. South-Western Educational Publishing disclaims any affiliation, association, connection with, sponsorship, or endorsement by such owners.

Preface

Welcome to Desktop Publishing

Advances in word processing software have made it easier for users to create documents with a *typeset*, not merely *typed*, appearance. Since the appearance of documents makes a strong first impression on readers (and potential customers), word processing students need to learn the tricks of the trade: how to use with efficiency and good judgment the advanced features of their word processing software. This text emphasizes basic skills in desktop publishing through a variety of modern, real-life activities. Students will develop skills key to the desktop publisher, including making design and typography decisions, handling multicolumn documents, inserting and editing graphics, and creating styles and charts. Students will create a portfolio of business documents, including a newsletter, to demonstrate their mastery of these skills.

This text may be used in a traditional classroom setting or in an individualized lab setting. The book is short, concise, and fun to work through. This book can be used as a basis for a desktop publishing class or as supplementary material in a variety of classes including: *keyboarding, business communications, journalism, office procedures, job readiness, and computer applications.*

Features

The ten chapters in *Desktop Publishing: 10-Hour Series* include
- A simple-to-complex approach to develop desktop publishing skills.
- Realistic, fun, and engaging business-related activities with easy-to-follow directions and solution models to ensure success.
- Instructions designed for a variety of word processing programs.
- Graphic tips to help develop effective desktop publishing skills.
- Fully explained graphic instructions for software clipart.
- On Your Own activities to be used as extensions of the regular instruction.

A template diskette (ISBN: 0-538-68756-8) containing text and graphics used in many of the activities completes the package of student materials.

The teacher's manual includes:
- Teaching suggestions.
- Quick review questions and answers.
- Course grading scale for use by both student and instructor.
- An objective and a production mid-term quiz and final exam.

Other books available in the *10-Hour Series* are
- *Composing at the Computer*
- *Power Business Reading*
- *Proofreading at the Computer*
- *On-line Resumés and Job Search*

Contents

1 Design for Focus and Flow — 2
- 1-1: Plan Your Document — 4
- 1-2: Determine Focus and Flow — 5

Design to Achieve Balance — 6
- 1-3: Evaluate a Document's Design — 8
- 1-4: On Your Own — 9

2 Insert/Modify Graphics — 10
- 2-1: Insert and Modify Clipart — 12
- 2-2: Insert Clipart from Disk — 12
- 2-3: Copy and Insert an Internet Graphic — 13
- 2-4: Copy and Insert an Internet Graphic Offline — 13

Enhance Graphic Images — 14
- 2-5: Add Border, Shadow, and Shade — 18
- 2-6: Wrap Text — 18
- 2-7: Create a Sale Ad — 19
- 2-8: On Your Own — 19

3 Edit Graphic Images I — 20
- 3-1: Crop Clipart — 24
- 3-2: Group, Rotate, and Flip Clipart — 24
- 3-3: Rotate and Flip Clipart — 24

Edit Graphic Images II — 26
- 3-4: Change Details of a Graphic Image — 28
- 3-5: Create an Invitation Using Modified Graphic Images — 29
- 3-6: On Your Own — 29

4 Choose Typography — 30
- 4-1: Use Font and Spacing Options — 32
- 4-2: Add Graphics — 32

Use Special Characters — 34
- 4-3: Insert Drop Caps and Bullets in an Article — 36
- 4-4: Use Special Characters in an Ad — 37

5 Create Columns — 38
- 5-1: Set Columns and Column Breaks — 40
- 5-2: Change Orientation and Column Widths — 40
- 5-3: Set Columns, Gutter Widths, and Column Breaks — 41

Improve the Look of Columns — 42
- 5-4: Create a Newsletter — 44
- 5-5: Enhance a Newsletter — 45

6 Use Drawing Tools, Lines, and Borders — 46
- 6-1: Use Basic Shapes, Text Boxes, and Page Border — 50
- 6-2: Use Preformatted Shapes — 50
- 6-3: On Your Own — 50

7 Create and Apply Styles — 52
- 7-1: Apply Styles — 54
- 7-2: Create and Apply Styles — 54
- 7-3: Create Styles — 55
- 7-4: On Your Own — 56

8 Present Numerical Information with Charts — 58
- 8-1: Create a Chart — 62
- 8-2: Create a Chart — 63
- 8-3: Insert a Chart — 64
- 8-4: On Your Own — 64

9 Add Special Effects — 66
- 9-1: Add Watermarks — 68
- 9-2: Use Words as Artwork — 69
- 9-3: On Your Own — 69

10 Create a Portfolio — 70
- 10-1: Create a Business Card — 70
- 10-2: Create an Ad — 71
- 10-3: Create a Drawing — 71
- 10-4: Create a Letterhead Template — 72
- 10-5: Format a Business Letter — 72
- 10-6: Create a Fax Cover Sheet and a Memo Form — 72
- 10-7: Create a Newsletter — 74
- 10-8: Create a Title Page — 74

Design for Focus and Flow

Focus

- Plan your document's design with five critical questions in mind.
- Observe how design elements create a focus point and visual flow in your document.

Planning

To produce documents with a professional appearance, the first step is to plan your document by answering five questions.

- What is the **purpose** of your publication? The design elements of the document should match the message that you want to communicate.

- Who is the **audience**? How much do they know or need to know about your topic?

- What will be the **form** of the publication? Will it be a single sheet, a tri-fold flyer, or a multipage report?

- What **content** will you include? In what form will the content be? How much text will be included? Will there be *graphic images* such as charts, graphs, or maps?

- How will you **distribute** your publication? Will it be folded and placed in an envelope, displayed on a bulletin board, or included with other documents?

The answer to each of these questions will affect your design decisions.

Focus and Flow

Developing a well-designed document means understanding the concepts of focus point and flow. The *focus point* is the element within the document that the reader sees first. Graphic images, type font or size, and white space can create the focus point. Type that is large, distinct, or colorful catches the reader's attention. *White space* is the "blank" area between elements and in the outside page margins. It requires careful placement and planning. White space gives the reader a "breather" and causes other elements to have greater impact.

When choosing a focus point, remember that the eye tends to see:

- Graphics before text.
- Larger text before smaller.
- Text in bright colors before text in black.

Once you have your reader's attention, you need to keep it. You can do this by creating a visual path or *flow* for the reader to follow. The flow enables the reader's eye to move easily from the focus point through the rest of the page in the order you intend the document to be read. The *Z pattern* is a commonly used visual path. The Z pattern starts at the top left of the page, moves to the top right, down to the bottom left, and then to the bottom right. In Figure 1 the Z pattern and movement from graphic to text and larger to smaller drive the design.

1. The large butterfly draws the eye to the top left.
2. The eye moves to the title of the book. The large-sized font used for the title helps pull the eye along.
3. Next, the eye moves to the publication information, which is smaller than the title information, and finally stops at the smaller butterflies.

Placement of graphics, white space, or large text can change the reader's starting place. One of these design elements may grab the reader's attention at the bottom of the page before the eye moves upward, or the eye may start at the middle of the page and move outward.

Figure 1

Activity 1-1: Plan Your Document

1. Discuss as a class how the document below demonstrates planning and addresses these five planning questions:

   Purpose? Notification of Meeting
   Audience? Garden Club Members
   Form? Flyer
   Content? Calendar
   Distribution? Bulletin Board

2. Use the handout provided by your teacher and identify how it also addresses the five planning questions.

Please Post			May			
Sun	**Mon**	**Tue**	**Wed**	**Thu**	**Fri**	**Sat**
	1	2	3	4	5	6
7	8	9	10	11	12	13
14	15	16	17 *Garden Club Meeting 8 p.m.*	18	19	20
21	22	23	24	25	26	27
28	29	30	31			

Mark your calendar. We need to plan our Summer Extravaganza of Roses.

Design for Focus and Flow

Activity 1-2: Determine Focus and Flow

1. Determine the focus and flow of each of the four designs. Number the elements of each illustration in the order in which they catch your eye. Number the focal point **1**, the next element that catches your eye **2**, and so forth. In the first design below, the butterfly is the first element to attract your eye, followed by the title information and then the publication information. The reader's eye is forced to move around the page.

2. Which of the designs do you think are most effective in conveying the information? Why? In the next part of this hour, you'll discover one reason why you made your choice.

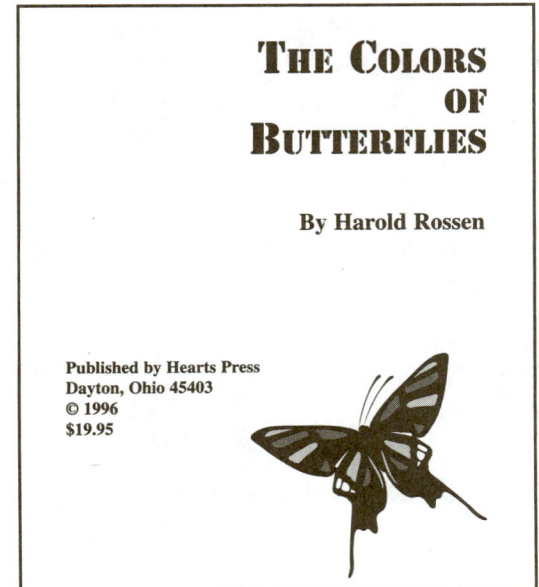

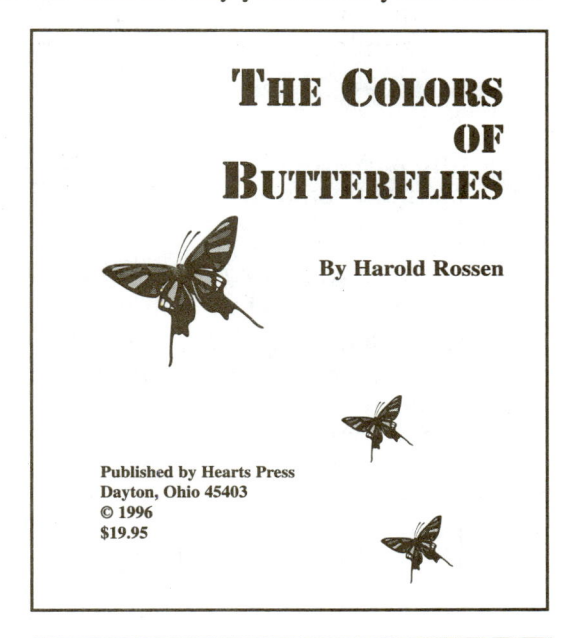

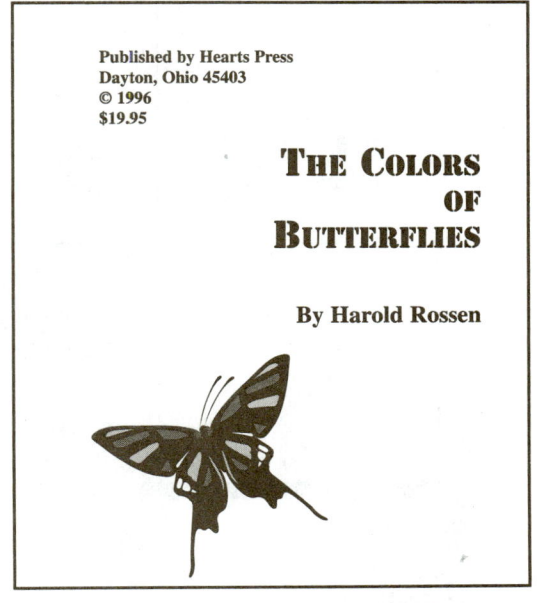

Design to Achieve Balance

Focus

- Design attractive documents by applying the principles of balance.

Symmetry

Focus and flow are not your only concerns when designing a page. The page must also be attractive to the eye. Use of symmetry is one way to achieve an attractive page because it gives a sense of consistency that is appealing. *Symmetry* requires that an element on one part of a page be balanced with another element. Elements such as graphics, text, and white space create a balance.

Figures 1 and 2 are divided into six sections. In Figure 1, text blocks balance sections 1 and 2. A graphic and a text block balance sections 3 and 4. A combination of the two elements balance sections 5 and 6. In Figure 2, the block of white space in section 2 balances the text block in section 1.

Asymmetrical pages contain elements that are not balanced against one another (*asymmetry*). While symmetrical pages are pleasing to the eye because of their consistency, asymmetrical pages appeal to our sense of novelty. The line of text "Call Betty" at the bottom of the page in Figure 2 is an asymmetrical block.

Figure 1 **Symmetrical**

Figure 2 **Asymmetrical**

The Rule of Thirds

Pages do not have to be divided evenly to be attractive. The "Rule of Thirds" states that it is more pleasing to view a page divided into thirds rather than halves. The division can be horizontal, vertical, or both. Figure 3 is divided horizontally into thirds.

Notice that several things are happening at once in Figure 3. White space in segment 2 balances the pharmaceutical symbol in segment 2. It also balances the store information in segment 3. In addition, each of the three segments acts as a balance against the others, providing a symmetry in threes.

The rule of thirds does not require a rigid division of a page into thirds. Notice that the store information in segment 3 does not fill the full third of the page.

Figure 4 shows the use of thirds in a vertical format and in halves horizontally. The white space in the upper middle segment balances the graphic below it. White space in the upper right segment balances text below it as well as the other white space. The lower text blocks are also in thirds.

Design options are endless. Recognizing the focus, flow, and balance of a page will help you design effective pages.

Figure 3

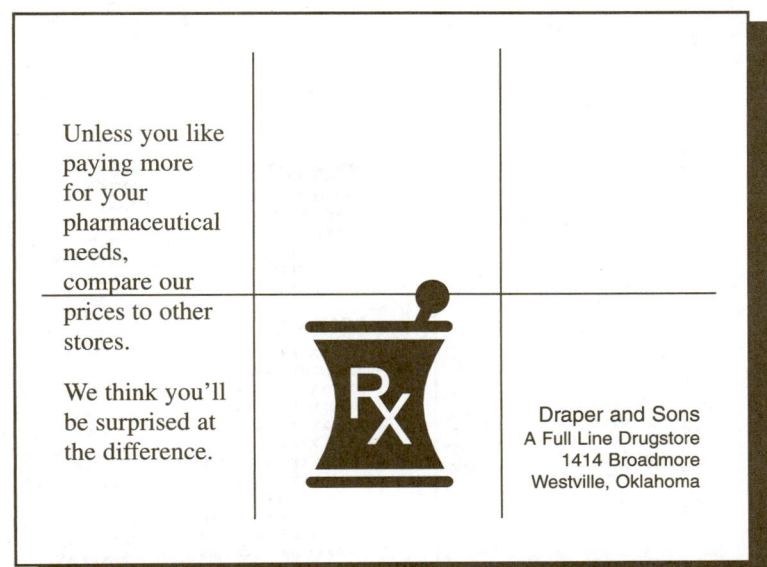

Figure 4

Design to Achieve Balance

Activity 1-3: Evaluate a Document's Design

1. Pencil in lines showing the division of the document vertically and horizontally in the figure below. Look for use of the rule of thirds and symmetry.
2. Identify each segment as text, white space, or graphic.
3. Draw arrows between segments that balance each other. Some segments may balance several other segments.
4. What is the focus point and how does your eye flow? Number each segment in order of your eye movement.
5. What would you do to improve the page for focus, flow, or balance?
6. Using the handout of this document, cut out and rearrange the segments to improve the design.
7. Which design do you like better? Why? Base your answer upon focus, flow, and balance.

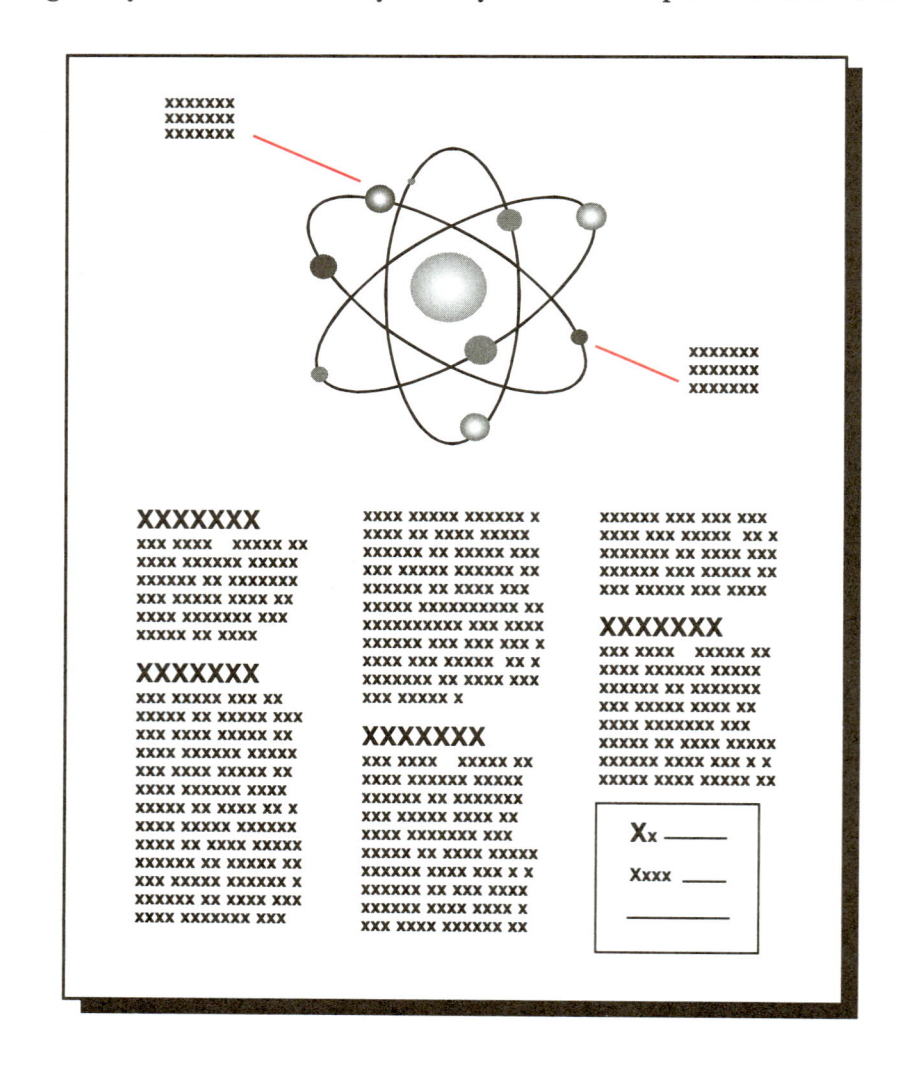

Activity 1-4: On Your Own

1. Using a copy of an ad from a magazine or newspaper, pencil in lines showing the division of the ad. Look for use of the rule of thirds and symmetry.

2. Identify each segment as text, white space, or graphic.

3. Draw arrows between segments that balance each other.

4. What is the focus point and how does your eye flow? Number each segment in order of your eye movement.

5. What would you do to improve the ad for focus, flow, or balance? Cut out each segment and rearrange the segments to restructure the ad's look. Draw a sketch showing the new arrangement.

6. Which design do you like better? Why? Base your answer upon focus, flow, and balance.

2 Insert/Modify Graphics

Focus

- Insert and modify graphics obtained from your software's clipart source and from the Internet.

Insert Graphic Images

Graphics draw attention to a page and enhance the meaning of the text. They should never be used just to decorate a page. When choosing a graphic, consider the content of the message and the intended audience. Ask yourself first, "Does this graphic add to my message or merely serve as filler?" and "Is my choice of art appropriate for my audience?"

An easy way to include graphics in your publication is with *clipart*. The term *clipart* is borrowed from the time when all publishing was paper-based (rather than computer-based), and graphics often were clipped from a clipart book. Today's word processing programs provide a selection of clipart. Additional graphics are available at reasonable cost on CD-ROM.

Another way to obtain graphic images is to copy photographs or drawings as graphic image files. You can import these files as graphics just as you import clipart images.

The Internet is also an excellent source of graphics. To use graphics from a World Wide Web site, you must copy the artwork to your computer's hard drive or a floppy disk.

To save a graphic from the Internet:

1. Create a folder called **Downloads**.

2. Right-click on a picture found on the Web. A drop-down menu will appear.

3. Choose *Save Image As* (or *Save Picture As*).

4. Key an appropriate file name or use the one provided. If you need to change the file format, key in *.bmp* after the file name (see *Graphic Tip*). Save in the **Downloads** folder. The graphic now can be imported into your document in a manner similar to clipart. Before importing your graphic, you may want to click on the Preview button located in the Insert or Import dialogue box to see what the graphic will look like.

Modify Graphics

Once a graphic image is inserted into a document, you can move it. Some software (for example, *Word 6*) requires you to place a frame around the graphic before you can move the graphic image. To frame the image, right-click on the image and select *Insert Frame*.

To move clipart:

1. Click on the clipart to select it. Small boxes (*handles*) will appear at the corners and along the side.

2. When the pointer changes to a 4-tipped arrow, hold down the mouse and drag the image to the new location. Release the mouse.

You can change the size of a graphic easily.

1. Select the graphic. Handles will appear.

2. Position the arrow on a corner and "push in" or "pull out" the handles to make the graphic smaller or larger. Use the corner handles to maintain the graphic's proportions. Using the handles along the side may change the proportion, making the picture wider, taller, narrower, or shorter.

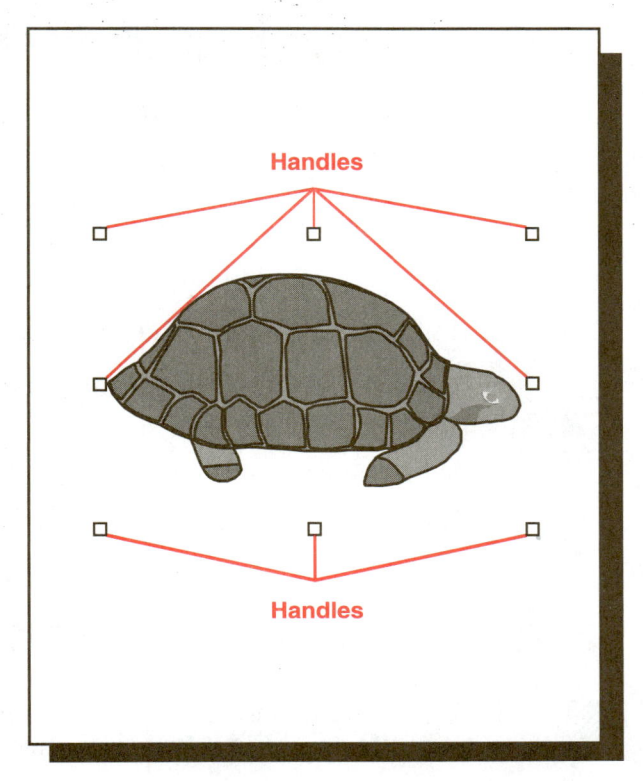

Figure 1

Graphic Tip

Graphic files are created using different programs. Each program saves the file in a different format, indicated by a three-letter code called an extension. Such extensions include .pcx, .bmp, .jpg, and .gif. Because Internet graphics are in .jpg or .gif formats, which some word processors do not import, you may need to save the graphic in a format that you can use; usually a .bmp format. See Appendix, p. 76, for more information on graphic file formats and extensions.

Using My Software

Access Help for functions and record the steps for your software.

SOFTWARE FUNCTIONS	STEPS
Insert clipart from word processor.	
Insert clipart as a scanned or Internet file.	

Insert/Modify Graphics

Activity 2-1: Insert and Modify Clipart

1. Open a blank document in your word processing program.
2. Insert any graphic image provided by your word processing program.
3. If necessary, insert a frame around the graphic.
4. Left-click outside the clipart to deselect it. Click on it again to select it.
5. Move the graphic to the lower right side of the page.
6. Change the size of the graphic using the corner handles. Change the size using one of the side handles.
7. With the graphic selected, press *Delete* or the *Backspace* key.
8. Repeat these steps until you are confident of the procedure.

Activity 2-2: Insert Clipart from Disk

1. Find the file **balloons** on the template disk and click once. Notice that it is in a .bmp format. Click *Preview* to see your selection.
2. Click *Insert* or *Open* to insert the graphic **balloons** into your document.
3. Click outside the balloons to return to your page or click *Close*. Select the balloons again and move them, resize them, and finally delete them.
4. Follow the same steps for **poodle**. Notice its file format.
5. Close the document without saving.

Balloons

Poodle

Activity 2-3: Copy and Insert an Internet Graphic

1. Open your Internet browser. Go to *http://www.swep.com*. From the main page, click on *Keyboarding & Office Tech*; choose *Keyboarding—Secondary*. Click on *Desktop Publishing in 10 Hours* and retrieve the file "Desktop Publishing in Ten Hours."

2. Right-click on the butterfly. From the drop-down menu, choose *Save Picture As* or *Save Image As*.

3. Name the picture **ACT2-3a.bmp** and save it to the **Downloads** folder you created earlier.

4. Browse the Internet for another graphic or use one from the template disk.

5. Save the new graphic as **ACT2-3b.bmp**.

6. Insert both new graphics into a new word processing document. Close without saving.

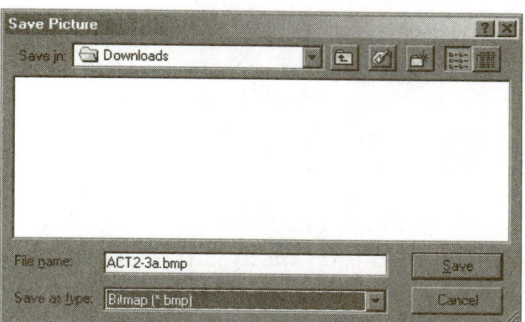

Optional Activity 2-4: Copy and Insert an Internet Graphic Offline

1. Open your Internet browser. Choose the option to work offline.

2. Open a blank browser screen. From the File menu, choose *Open* or *Open File in Browser*.

3. Locate **Desktop Publishing in Ten Hours** on your template disk. Click *Open* and the page will appear.

4. Right-click on the butterfly. From the drop-down menu, choose *Save Picture As* or *Save Image As*.

5. Name the picture **ACT2-4a.bmp** and save it to the **Downloads** folder.

6. Insert another graphic from the page.

7. Save the new graphic as **ACT2-4b.bmp**.

8. Insert both new graphics into a new word processing document. Close without saving.

Enhance Graphic Images

Focus

- Enhance graphics by wrapping text, adding borders, and adding shadows.

File Formats

Adding special effects such as borders and shadows to graphic images is a fun and easy way to customize your document. The file format of the image affects how you go about wrapping text and adding shadows and borders. File format also affects the final appearance of the graphic. Graphic file formats fall into two basic categories: bitmap and vector.

- *Bitmap* graphics are created or "painted" using small squares called pixels. *Pixels* create a "map" of the image. Figure 1 shows a triangle drawn as a bitmap and then enlarged to reveal the pixels used to paint it. Graphics that you scan, copy from the Internet, or create using the Windows Paint program are bitmaps.

- *Vector* graphics are drawn as mathematically defined segments rather than in tiny pieces. The triangle in Figure 2 consists of three segments, which have been drawn as a vector and enlarged ten times. Notice that each side of the triangle is a single unit. Often, the clipart images that come with word processors are vector graphics.

The Appendix on p. 76 lists a variety of bitmap and vector graphic file extensions and the programs used to create them.

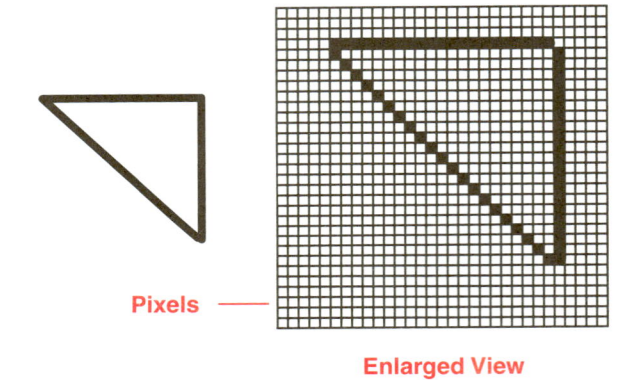

Pixels

Enlarged View

Figure 1   Bitmap

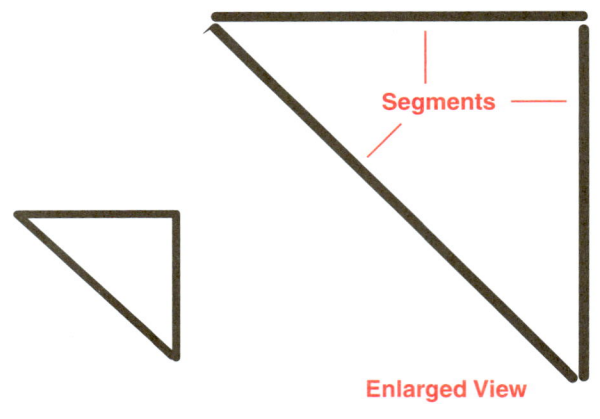

Segments

Enlarged View

Figure 2   Vector

Wrapping Text

Words and pictures can be integrated into a single block by "wrapping" text around a graphic. You can make text flow down the side and below the graphic by setting the amount of space between the graphic and the text.

- With vector graphics, it is possible to wrap text to follow the outline of the graphic, as shown in Figure 3.

- With bitmap graphics, text is squared off around an invisible rectangular outline as shown in Figure 4.

- Wrapping text around graphics can be overused. Avoid disrupting the continuity of a paragraph by positioning a graphic in the center of the paragraph. The graphic should instead be placed at the top or bottom edge of a column or between two columns.

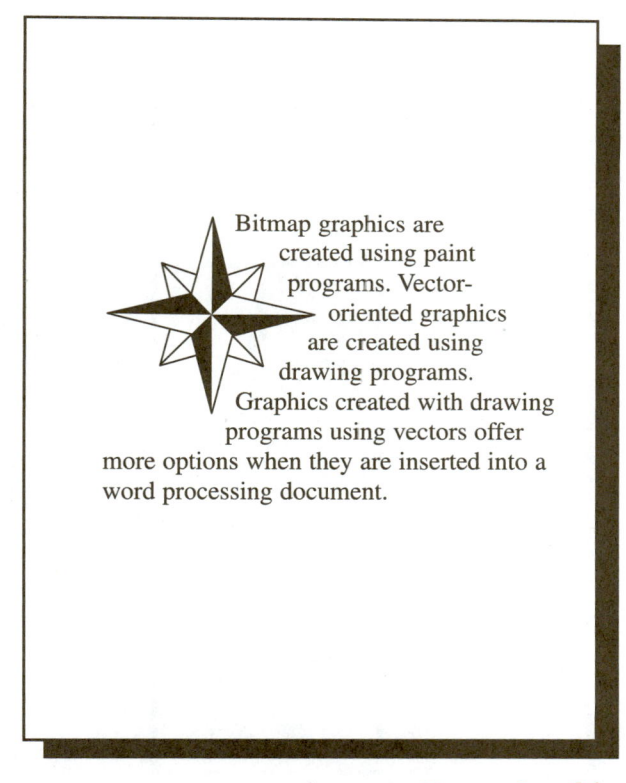

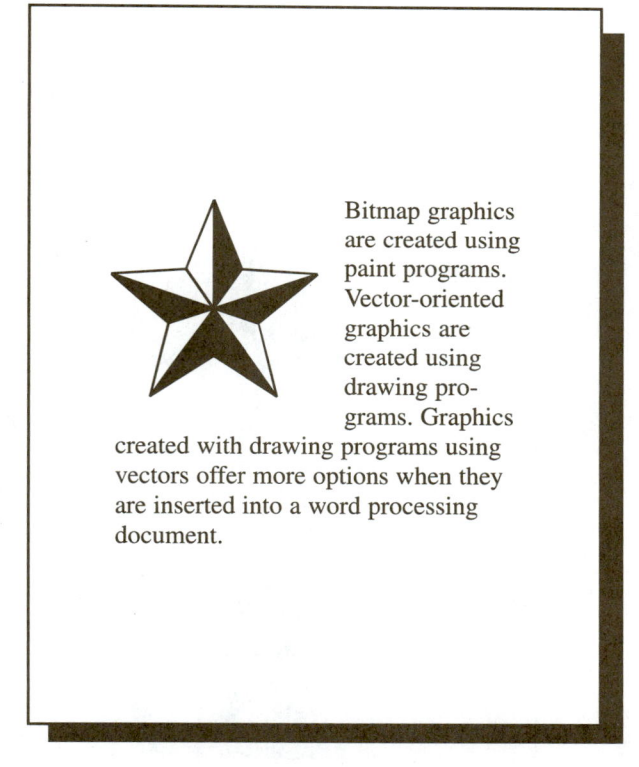

Figure 3 Vector Graphic

Figure 4 Bitmap Graphic

Enhance Graphic Images

Shadows

Creating a shadow around your graphic gives it a three-dimensional effect (Figure 5).

- With vector graphics, the shadow will attach itself to the actual figure.
- With bitmap graphics, the invisible rectangle around the figure will be given the shadow (Figure 5).

Borders

Adding a border around a graphic separates it from text (Figure 6).

- Border lines are measured in points. There are 72 points to an inch.
- A 6-point line is 1/12th of an inch wide (6/72 pts = 1/12").
- Borders can be black or a color.

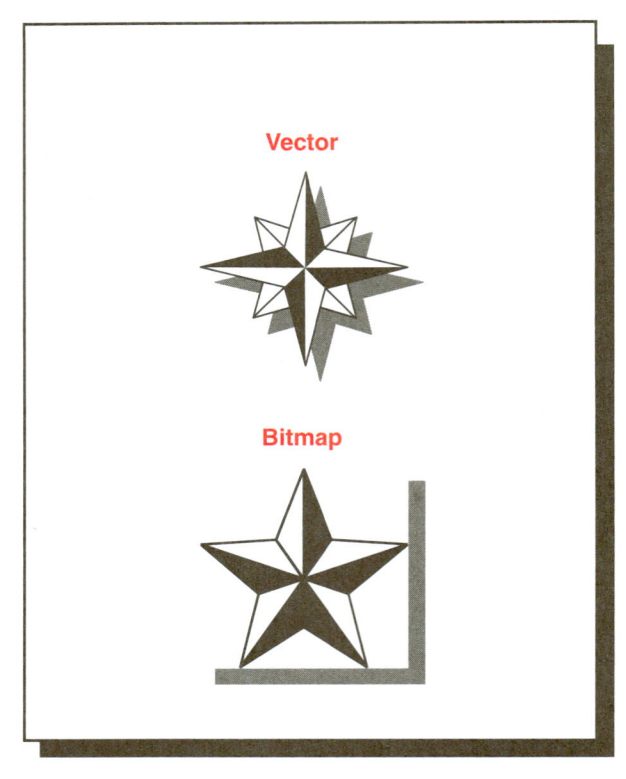

Figure 5   Shadows

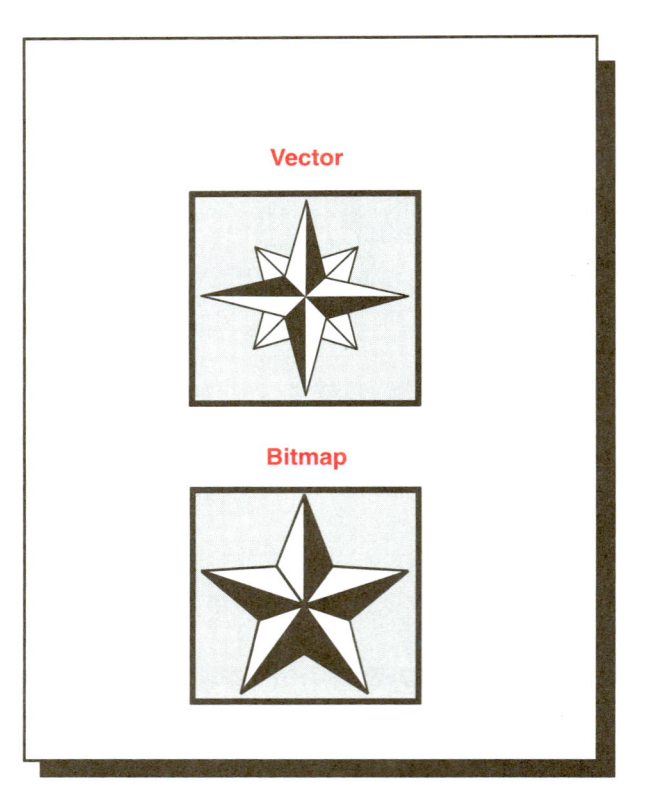

Figure 6   Borders/Shading

Enhance Graphic Images

Shading

You can also fill the area between the border and the graphic with a color or shade.

- Shading is measured in percentages from 5% to 100%. The higher the percentage, the darker the shade (see Figure 7).

- Shades can range from gray to black or can be in color. Shading can be effective as a means of separating your graphic from the surrounding text. It also adds impact to a graphic that might be lost in text.

- Shading will only work with a vector graphic as shown in Figure 6. It will not appear in a bitmap graphic even if a shade is selected.

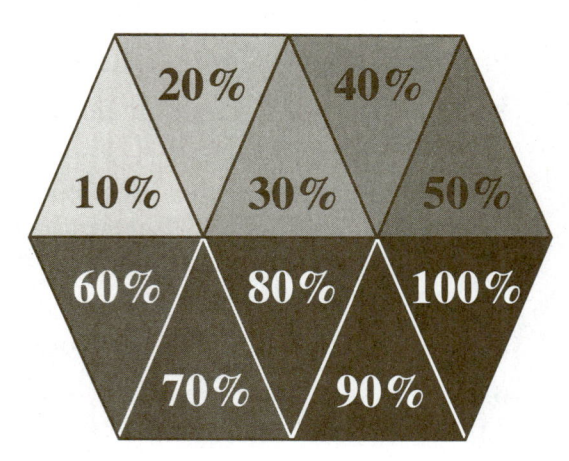

Figure 7

Graphic Tip

Any time you use someone else's artwork, you must be aware of copyright issues. This includes artwork you have scanned, artwork you copy from the Internet, and some clipart. Copyrights protect an artist's work by providing ownership. Because of this ownership, the artist can require payment if you use the work. Clipart may be royalty free, meaning you can use it in your publication without making any additional payment after the initial purchase. However, the artist still retains ownership.

Using My Software

Access Help for functions and record the steps for your software.

SOFTWARE FUNCTIONS	STEPS
Wrap text.	
Add shadows.	
Add borders.	
Add shading.	

Enhance Graphic Images

17

Activity 2-5: Add Border, Shadow, and Shade

1. Insert as a picture **star** from the template disk. It has a .wpg extension, indicating vector format.
2. Place a shadow around the graphic.
3. Place a 6-point dark blue border around the star.
4. Fill the graphic with a pale blue shade. Set the shading to 20% if you have the option. Notice that now the border, not the star, has the shadow.
5. Deselect the star by clicking outside the graphic.
6. Insert as a picture **roses** from the template disk. Notice that **roses** has a .bmp extension, indicating bitmap format.
7. Select the flower. Move the flower image if necessary. Add a shadow. Notice that the shadow is not connected to the rose, but to the box defining the graphic.
8. Add a 3-point green border and a light green shade to the rose. Notice that the background doesn't fill as the star did because the rose is a bitmap graphic.
9. Do not close the document. Move to Activity 2-6.

Activity 2-6: Wrap Text

1. Select the rose and change its size to about 2" wide, using the corner handle to maintain proportions. Repeat for the star.
2. Remove borders, shading, and shadows from both graphics, using the same functions used to add them. Choose the no-fill, no-border option.
3. Choose the text wrap option that will wrap text tightly on all sides.
4. Add this text in 20-point type, breaking the lines as shown:

   Spring flowers and stars bring joy to the heart.
   They appear when all hope is gone and renew our belief in nature.
   Without them, the world would be a drearier place.

5. Move the graphics around and note how the text re-wraps with each move.
6. Follow the same steps using the star. Notice how much closer the star wraps because it is a vector image. Close the file without saving.

Activity 2-7: Create a Sale Ad

1. Key the ad text in 14-point Times New Roman, breaking lines as shown.
2. From the template disk, insert the file **bike**.
3. Change the size (maintain proportions) so the bike image is 1" wide. Use the ruler on your screen to check the size.
4. Set text to wrap tightly.
5. Set the border at approximately 4 points, red, and include a shadow similar to that shown at right.
6. Save the document as **ACT2-7** and print it.
7. Using your printout, observe the visual flow of the ad. What element attracts your attention first? How effective is the arrangement of text and graphic?

FOR SALE

One slightly used bike.
Tires recently patched.
Call Joey at 555-0100
Tuesdays after 5 p.m.

Activity 2-8: On Your Own

1. Using your new skills, create a cover for a report similar to that shown at right. Remember the five planning questions: **purpose, audience, form, content, distribution**. Consider the location of your focal point.
2. Include at least one graphic from your clipart selection or the Internet.
3. Wrap text around the graphic using a border, shadow, and shading as needed. Be careful not to overuse them.
4. Save the document as **ACT2-8** and print it.

Desktop Publish Your Family History

Stefan Peterson

A quick and easy way to learn to use your word processing software to create a family history that will endure forever.

Smith-Jackson Publishing, Inc.

Enhance Graphic Images

3 Edit Graphic Images I

Focus

- Crop graphic images and rotate and flip vector graphic images.

Cropping

Cropping an image removes distracting parts, emphasizes important elements, and helps fit an image to the available space in a document. Compare the images in Figure 1 to see how cropping works. The original image (A) is uncropped and has a balanced horizontal and vertical orientation.

In B, the image has been cropped vertically. This crop forces the viewer's eye to move upward and emphasizes the vertical nature of a few flower stems. Now the image fits into a narrower space, making it a useful element in a page designed according to the rule of thirds.

In C, the image is cropped horizontally. This crop forces the viewer's eye to move left to right and emphasizes the overall arrangement of the flowers. Removing the pot also gives the flowers a sense of floating on the page.

Use cropping as a design tool by choosing the elements with the most impact, and then cropping around them. Be careful, however, not to crop out essential parts of the image. Doing so might prove distracting to your reader. For example, in a mountain view, missing tree tops might give your reader a sense of missing part of the picture.

A   B   C

Figure 1

Grouping

Rotating or flipping a vector graphic is possible once you understand how to *group* the segments that make up the graphic. Grouping allows you to format multiple segments as a single unit. Grouping a graphic is accomplished in one of two ways, depending on your software:

- After selecting the graphic, choose *Ungroup* from the Drawing menu and then immediately choose *Group*. With this action, the flipping and rotating options become active.

  or

- Double-click on the graphic to go into an editing window similar to Figure 2. Once in the editing window, you can see the segments that make up the vector image. Each segment is defined by "points" (small squares). Using the pointer tool, create a large selection rectangle around all the segments (or choose *Select All*). Notice that some points of a segment are located a distance from the visual part of the segment. Be sure to "gather in" all the points in your selection rectangle.

  Once the segments are selected, the Group tool creates a single object with its own set of points. Figure 3 illustrates that the house has been grouped and is now a unit with points indicating a single segment. Now you can edit the house as a unit to rotate or flip it.

  Choosing Ungroup will return the graphic image to a series of points rather than just one segment.

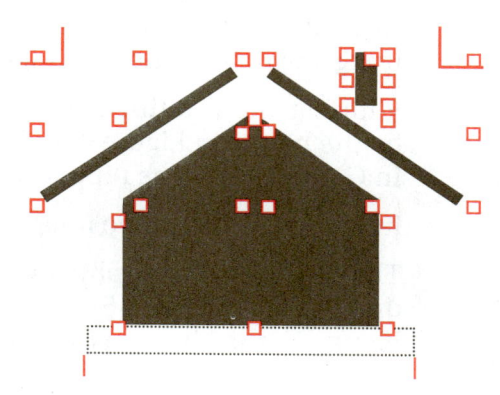

Figure 2   Ungrouped Image

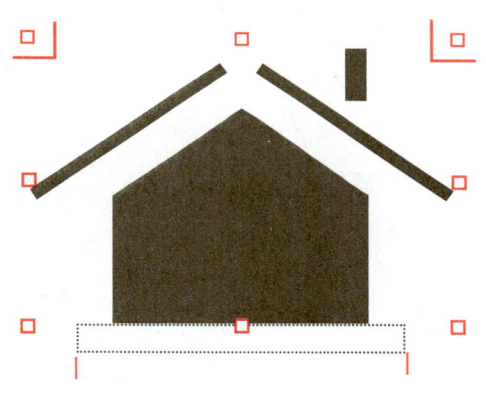

Figure 3   Grouped Image

Edit Graphic Images I

Rotate/Flip Graphics

Now that you know how to group your segments, you can easily rotate and flip vector graphic images.

Your software may allow you to rotate a vector graphic freely in small increments or only in 45- or 90-degree increments. Graphics are flipped either horizontally (from side to side) or vertically (from top to bottom). You may also have the option to create a mirror image, which is a horizontal flip.

Flipping and rotating allows the same picture to be used several ways, as demonstrated by the hands in Figure 4. In B, the hand was flipped horizontally and is a mirror image. In C, the image was flipped vertically from top to bottom.

In Figures 5 and 6, the images were rotated to the right and left and then incrementally.

The position of a graphic image affects the movement of the reader's eye. The rotated dragonflies in Figure 5 cause the eye to move in a circular motion. The watermelons in Figure 6 cause the eye to move from left to right.

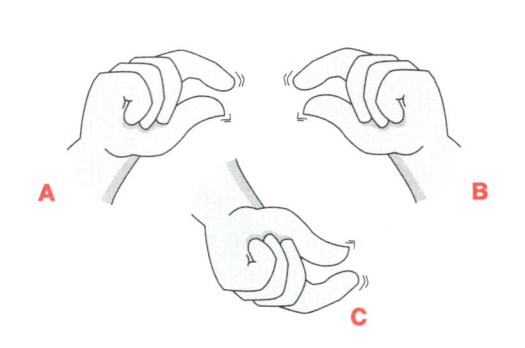

Figure 4   Flipping

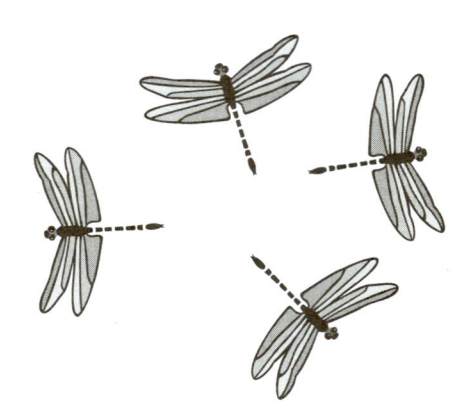

Figure 5   Rotating

Figure 6   Rotating

Edit Graphic Images I

Graphic Tip

Since only vector graphics can be rotated and flipped, you may need to determine what type of graphic images you have available. To find the extension of a graphic file, use the Insert File option rather than the clipart option. A dialogue box will appear, listing all the files in a particular folder and showing the extension of each.

Using My Software

Access Help for functions and record the steps for your software.

SOFTWARE FUNCTIONS	STEPS
Crop graphics.	
Group graphics.	
Rotate graphics.	
Flip graphics.	

Activity 3-1: Crop Clipart

1. Insert a clipart graphic. **Tip:** Look in the graphics or clipart folder of your word processing program to locate the clipart.
   Alternately: Use the graphics you copied from the Internet and saved to the **Downloads** folder.
2. Practice cropping from one side. From the Edit menu, select *Undo*.
3. Crop from the opposite side.
4. Crop the top and bottom. Undo after each action.
5. Crop your graphic to give it the most impact. Where is your eye focusing?
6. Delete the graphic. Leave the file open for the next activity.

Activity 3-2: Group, Rotate, and Flip Clipart

1. Insert a clipart file. Choose a graphic that has an obvious right and left orientation to make the flip from left to right more noticeable.
2. Depending on your software, choose *Ungroup* and then *Group*, or go into the editing window to select all your points and then choose *Group*.
3. Rotate the graphic right and then left. After each rotation, undo your work.
4. Next, flip the graphic from side to side and then top to bottom, undoing after each action.
5. Can you think of a situation when this would be helpful?
6. Close the document without saving.

Activity 3-3: Rotate and Flip Clipart

1. Open a new blank page with 1" margins.
2. Insert **sports figures** from the template disk.
3. Crop the graphic, leaving only the soccer player.
4. Insert **sports figures** again and crop, leaving the basketball player.
5. Repeat the process, leaving the tennis player.
6. Insert **football** and group the segments if necessary.

7. Copy the image and paste twice so there are three footballs.
8. Rotate one football at least 90 degrees. Flip one of the footballs. Place all three at the top of the page.
9. Set all the graphics to No Wrap.
10. Key the text in any 36-point font. Make the heading slightly larger.
11. Bold and center the title; right-align the text.
12. Save the flyer as **ACT3-3** and print it.

Edit Graphic Images II

Focus

■ Alter color and details of vector graphics.

Details and Colors

You can further change the graphics provided by your word processing program by altering the color or details. When you alter details and colors of these files, you actually move, delete, change the color of and add shadows to the segments that make up the image. Figures 1–5 illustrate each of these actions. Notice that the points defining the segment are visible whenever a segment is being modified.

To modify vector graphics, some word processing software requires you to double-click to go into an editing window. Other word processing software requires you to ungroup the segments first. In both cases, a special toolbar with graphic editing options becomes available.

- To move a segment, click on it and move it while holding down the left mouse button.

- To change a segment, click on it and choose the color or shadow option.

- To delete a segment, select it and press *Delete* or *Backspace*.

- To change the color of a segment or to add a shadow, use the toolbar.

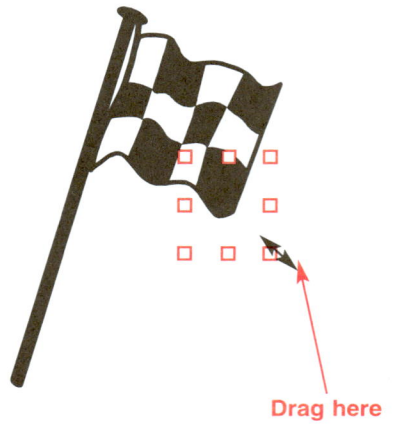

Drag here

Figure 1

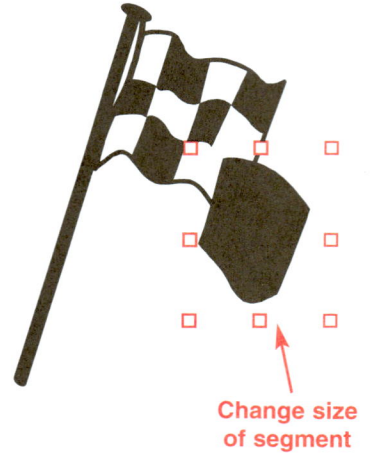

Change size of segment

Figure 2

Because the segments consist of a series of points, you can change the shape or size of a segment by dragging one of the points. Points look and function just like handles of a graphic. Place your cursor on a point. When the pointer changes to a double-sided arrow, drag the arrow to resize the segment.

To change several segments at once, group the segments first. Use the grouping method you learned in the previous lesson to select just the segments you want to alter.

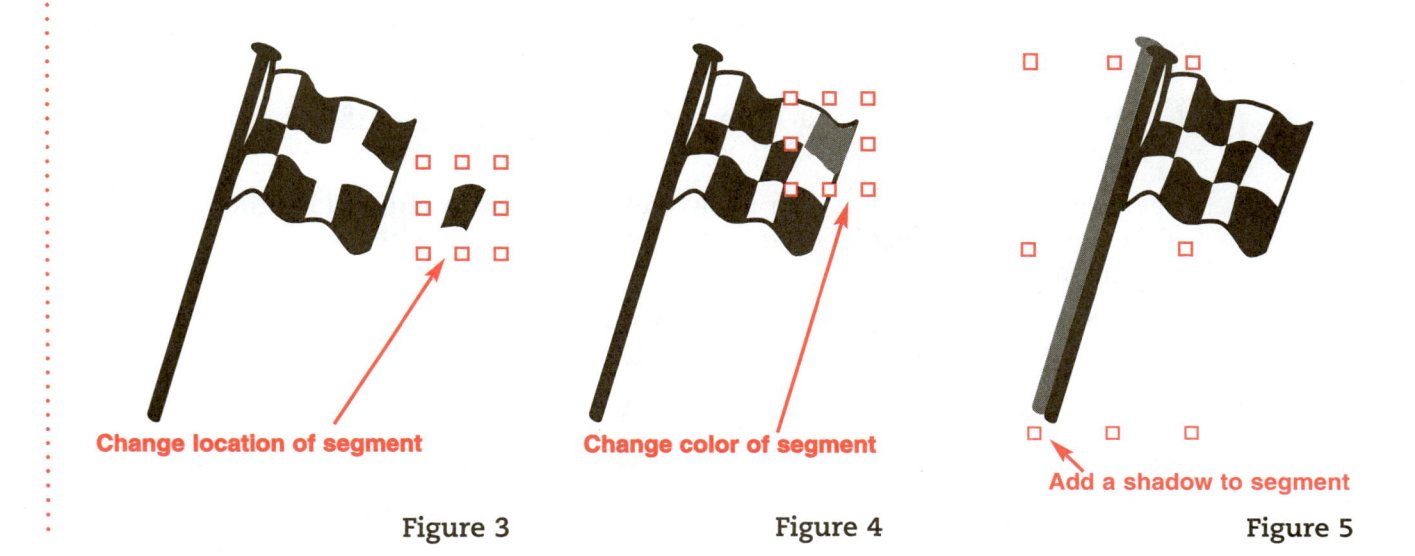

Change location of segment

Change color of segment

Add a shadow to segment

Figure 3　　　　　　　　Figure 4　　　　　　　　Figure 5

Using My Software

Access Help for functions and record the steps for your software.

SOFTWARE FUNCTIONS	STEPS
Edit vector graphics.	
List toolbar choices.	

Edit Graphic Images II

Activity 3-4: Change Details of a Graphic Image

1. Insert **cat** from the template file. Ungroup the graphic or double-click to go into an editing window.

2. Select segment A (as shown below) and delete it. Delete segments B–D that make up the background of the cat's face, leaving only the facial features. You may have to delete both the outline and the color to remove the entire shape.

3. Delete segment E around the cat's tongue. Select the tongue and change its color to orange. Change slightly the shape of the tongue by dragging one of the vector points. Your drawing will be similar to the one on the right.

4. Move the inside of the cat's ear (F) away from the face. Notice that the outline does not move.

5. Select the inside of the other ear (G) as well as the border around it. Shift-click or lasso to select both pieces. Group the two pieces and move them as a unit away from the face.

6. Change the placement of the whiskers by moving the lines that make up the whiskers. Change the width and color of the whisker lines.

7. Make other fun changes. Perhaps change the cat's eye color to blue.

8. If necessary, click outside the editing window or close the window to return to your page.

9. Close the document without saving.

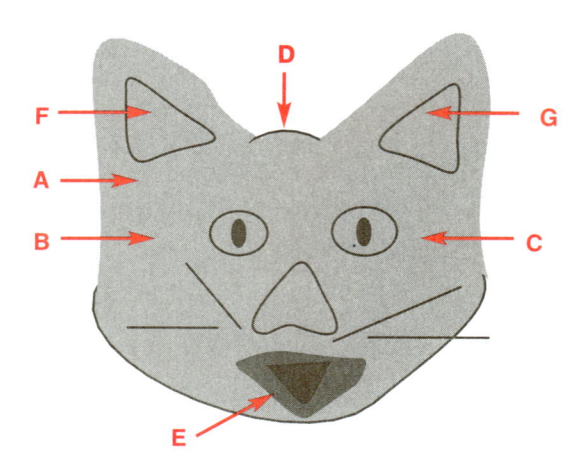

Edit Graphic Images II

Activity 3-5: Create an Invitation Using Modified Graphic Images

1. In a new document, key the invitation text (shown below), beginning each line at the left margin.
2. Insert the file **elephant**.
3. Ungroup the illustration. Remove the body of the elephant leaving only the ear, head, and trunk.
4. Lasso the remaining parts using the pointer tool. Group the segments. Flip the image horizontally so the elephant faces right. Rotate the picture slightly to raise the elephant's trunk.
5. Change the elephant's color from gray to something brighter. Reduce the elephant's size to about 2" wide.
6. Place a shadow around the elephant. Set the text to wrap tightly around the elephant.
7. Place the elephant in the left corner of the invitation.
8. Insert a picture of a donkey from the Internet or your own clipart selection. Change its size to about 1.5" wide. Crop, reposition, and edit the image as necessary.
9. Save the invitation as **ACT3-5** and print it.

> It's an election. Whom did you vote for?
> We don't care.
> Democrats   Republicans
> All are welcome at our election night party.
> Your voter registration card will be your ticket.
> The party starts as soon as the polls close.

Activity 3-6: On Your Own

1. Create an 8 1/2" x 11" poster using a saying or motto that appeals to you.
2. Insert graphics that reinforce the message.
3. Modify the graphics using cropping, rotating, modifying details, changing colors, and wrapping the text.
4. Save the poster as **ACT3-6** and print it.

Edit Graphic Images II

4 Choose Typography

Focus

- Enhance the appearance of your documents with typography choices.

Typography

In the past, whenever you picked the *font* (style and size of type) to use in a letter or report, you made a decision about typography perhaps without realizing it. *Typography* describes the arrangement and appearance of type on a page, which includes the size and style of a font as well as its attributes and spacing.

Up to now, you may have chosen your typography simply on the need to fit a certain amount of text on a single page. In desktop publishing, typography choices are made for visual appeal, adding power to the text's message.

Fonts

Font styles fall into three basic categories (see Figure 1): *serif*, *sans serif*, and *fancy*.

- Serif fonts have small "feet" or *serifs* attached to letters. Serif fonts such as Times Roman are frequently used for body copy.

- Sans serif fonts do not have serifs. Arial is a sans serif font often used for headings and large type.

- Fancy fonts may or may not have serifs, but they are ornate or specialized. Use fancy fonts for special display purposes such as invitations.

The organization and relative importance of text within the document determines the size of type you choose.

- Use larger type for headings and titles. Allow extra space above and below headings.
- Use smaller type for subheadings.
- Use the smallest type (10-12 points) for body text.

Serif
32 pt. Times

Sans serif
32 pt. Helvetica

Fancy
44 pt. Kaufmann

Figure 1

Graphic Tip

All caps in a document tend to "scream" the message. If you need to use all caps, consider using the small caps attribute instead. It will deliver your message in a normal tone of voice.

Attributes

Attributes are typographical features such as bold, italic, and underline, as well as small caps, shadow, and color. Reverse type—using white text on a dark background—is created using the color attribute. A good designer applies attributes sparingly.

Spacing

Consider these three spacing elements as you make typography decisions for your documents:

- *Line spacing* is the vertical space between lines of body copy. The usual choices are single, 1.5 spaces, or double.

- Spacing before and after a paragraph is the amount of space between paragraphs rather than between the lines of body copy. It can be set in points or as spaces. Frequently, if body copy is set for single spacing, spacing before and after paragraphs is set at 1.5 spaces to give a visual break between paragraphs.

- In desktop publishing, the convention is to use a single space after terminal punctuation rather than two spaces.

Finally, when you are making font choices, keep in mind that fonts serve to organize text. Too many font styles, sizes, and attributes clutter a page and may confuse your reader. No more than four changes in font type should occur on a single page.

Using My Software

Access Help for functions and record the steps for your software.

SOFTWARE FUNCTIONS	STEPS
Choose font style, size, and attributes.	
Set line spacing.	
Set spacing before and after a paragraph.	
Create reverse type.	

Choose Typography

Activity 4-1: Use Font and Spacing Options

1. From your word processing software, open the template file **FFD**. Refer to the illustration on page 33.

2. Select all the text on the page and change it to a 12-point serif type. Try other serif font choices and choose one that is readable and effective.

3. Select the title. Center the title and change its font size to at least 24 points. Choose a different style of font.

4. Set the title background to black and the font color to white. This creates a reverse-type title.

5. Choose small caps and bold type for the text of the title.

6. Increase the size of the subheadings to 14 points and make them bold.

7. Set the spacing to 1.5 between the subheading and the body text below.

8. Leave the document open for the next activity.

Activity 4-2: Add Graphics

1. Insert **cans** from the template disk.

2. Copy and paste the graphic twice.

3. Reduce the size of the cans, making them about 1.5" tall.

4. Rotate the cans similar to the illustration on page 33. Remember to group them first.

5. The Wrap Text option should be used if available.

6. Save the document as **ACT4-2** and print it.

7. Evaluate your printout. How does your font choice affect the instructional sheet? How does the use of the cans create a focus?

FEED THE FAMILIES DAY ← 24 pts.

The food drive is scheduled for November 1. We ← 12 pts.
appreciate everyone's help in this important event. Follow the guidelines below to help us run the drive smoothly and to maximize community contributions. Please feel free to contact Shirley Hudson at 555-1133 if you have any questions or encounter any difficulties.

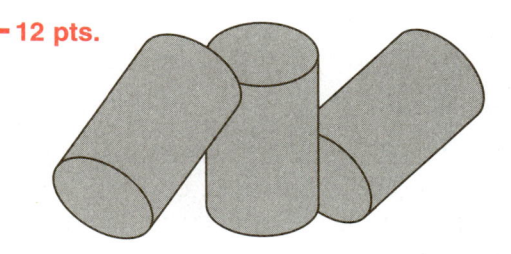

Hand out Flyers ← 14 pts.

Flyers will be available beginning October 15. You can pick them up at the district office. They will be packaged in bundles of 100. Please take as many as you think you can hand out. Be optimistic in your estimate. The flyers should be distributed the weekend preceding the food drive. Remember that the flyers cannot be placed in mailboxes. Instead, place them on the windshields of parked cars or inside the front doors of homes. Work in pairs. It's safer and more fun.

Our goal is to blanket the city with the flyers! When you pick up your flyers, you will indicate on a map the area that you will cover, so think about this before you arrive. Again, be optimistic, but realistic, about the ground you can cover. We know from experience that our volunteers sometimes overestimate their abilities. If you find you can't complete distributing the flyers in your area, call the office as soon as possible so that we can reassign your area.

Tell the Story

Verbal "flyers" are frequently more effective than printed ones. Tell everyone you see about the event and answer their questions as you distribute the flyers in your area. Keep these facts in mind as you tell people about the event:

* Feed the Families Day was started in 1986.
* We collected over 100,000 pounds of food last year.
* The food is distributed to local agencies.
* There will be drop-off points at many local businesses.

On the Day

On November 1, a semi-trailer donated for our use by Gordon Moorefield Trucking will pick up the donated food at several local businesses. We need volunteers to help sort the food and load it on the truck. Let us know when you pick up your flyers if you want to help also with the food loading. We ask that volunteers sign up for two-hour shifts beginning at 6 a.m. and ending at 10 p.m.

Use Special Characters

Focus

▪ Use special characters that add visual information and flair to your documents.

Special Characters

Word processing software allows you easy access to special characters such as mathematical symbols, copyright/trademark symbols, fancy bullets, arrows, and so forth. Numerous options are available depending upon the font or set that is selected.

Most word processing software has a menu selection that allows you to insert special characters. For those that do not, the Character Map, found under Accessories in the Program menu, offers the same features. To use the map, you have to copy the symbol and then paste it into your document.

Dingbats. A *dingbat* is a symbol such as the star shown in Figure 1. It is inserted as text but is actually a graphic. Dingbats are frequently gathered into a single font selection called Wingdings, Dingbats, Symbols, etc.

Diacritical markings. Diacritical markings in a word indicate how parts of a word are pronounced. Used properly, diacritical marks add clarity to your work. The word résumé shows the use of diacritical marks.

Property symbols. A trademark™, registered trademark ®, or a copyright © symbol is a cross between a dingbat and type and is used to indicate specific legal rights. The use of these symbols rather than the words will make your work look more professional.

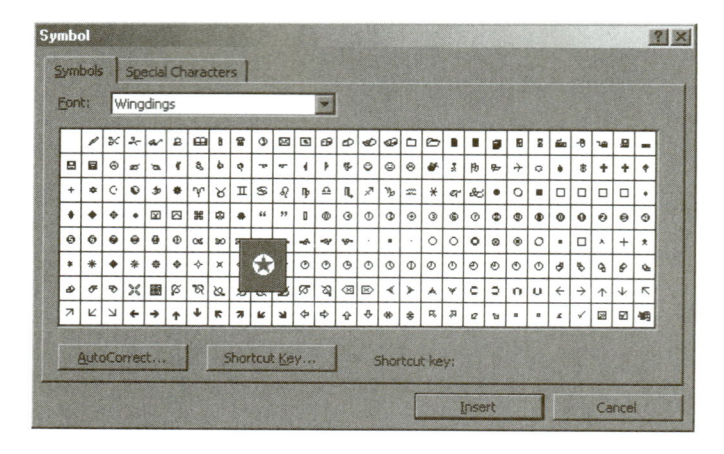

Figure 1

Other Special Characters

Bullets. *Bullets* add emphasis to a list. Most word processing software packages have options to create bullets automatically, making bulleted lists easy to use.

- Bullets can draw the eye to a list, adding impact.
- Bullets can be large dots.
- Bullets can be graphics.

Using dingbats instead of standard circular bullets adds interest to a list. Notice in the example above that the bullets are set off from the text with a hanging indent and that additional space (6 points or 1.5 spaces) is placed between items on the list. Both of these options enhance the appearance of a bulleted list.

Smart quotes. *Smart quotes* (" ") are curly quotation marks inserted automatically by word processing programs. Straight quotes may be used to indicate inches and seconds. Generally, straight quotes are available from the Symbols dialog box.

Drop caps. *Drop caps* are larger, enhanced first letters of a paragraph. Drop caps are easy to create and can be used effectively as an opening for initial paragraphs in documents.

Drop caps may be set to drop down any number of lines, but three lines is most common. The text can be set to start at the top, middle, or bottom of the cap. Because a drop cap indicates the beginning of a new paragraph, do not indent the paragraph in which it occurs.

> A drop cap can add a touch of class to any document. Most drop caps take up three lines. The paragraph is not indented because the drop cap signals a new paragraph.

Figure 2

Using My Software

Access Help for functions and record the steps for your software.

SOFTWARE FUNCTIONS	STEPS
Create special bullets.	
Insert drop caps.	

Use Special Characters

Activity 4-3: Insert Drop Caps and Bullets in an Article

1. Create a new document with a 1" left margin and a 5.5" right margin to create a column effect.
2. Key in the information shown in the illustration below using a 10-point font.
3. Insert a drop cap in the first paragraph.
4. Create bullets as shown.
5. Save the newsletter article as **ACT4-3** and print it.

> **W**hat a year! By the time you receive this newsletter, there will only be a few more weeks of school left. Summer vacation is just around the corner.
>
> I would like to thank each of you for your support and interest in our new "Reach the Kids" program. We appreciate the involvement of our community in this venture. Without each of you, we would not have been successful in reducing our drop-out rate significantly.
>
> Mark your calendars for the following closing events:
>
> ❏ Recognition Ceremony Monday, May 15 at 7 p.m.
> ❏ All School Day at the Park Thursday, May 25 from 8 a.m. to 4 p.m.
>
> I look forward to seeing all of you at these events and in September. Have a great summer!
>
> Anna Johnson, Dean of Students

Activity 4-4: Use Special Characters in an Ad

1. Open a blank word processing document with 1.5" margins.
2. Key in text shown in the ad below except for the special characters and bullets. Use only a single space after punctuation marks.
3. Set the quote from Recording Magazine in a 26-point font; right-align "Recording Magazine."
4. Set the first paragraph and bulleted information in an 18-point font.
5. Change "Jaime's CD Exchange" to an attractive sans serif font, and place a registered symbol ® after "Mirror Recordings."
6. Use check marks to create the bulleted list.
7. With symbols, create a line to divide the address from the list above it. You may increase the font size to make the symbol more visible. Center the symbols line.
8. Set the address information to a 14-point sans serif font, centered. Use symbols to break up business information as shown.
9. Save the ad as **ACT4-4** and print it.

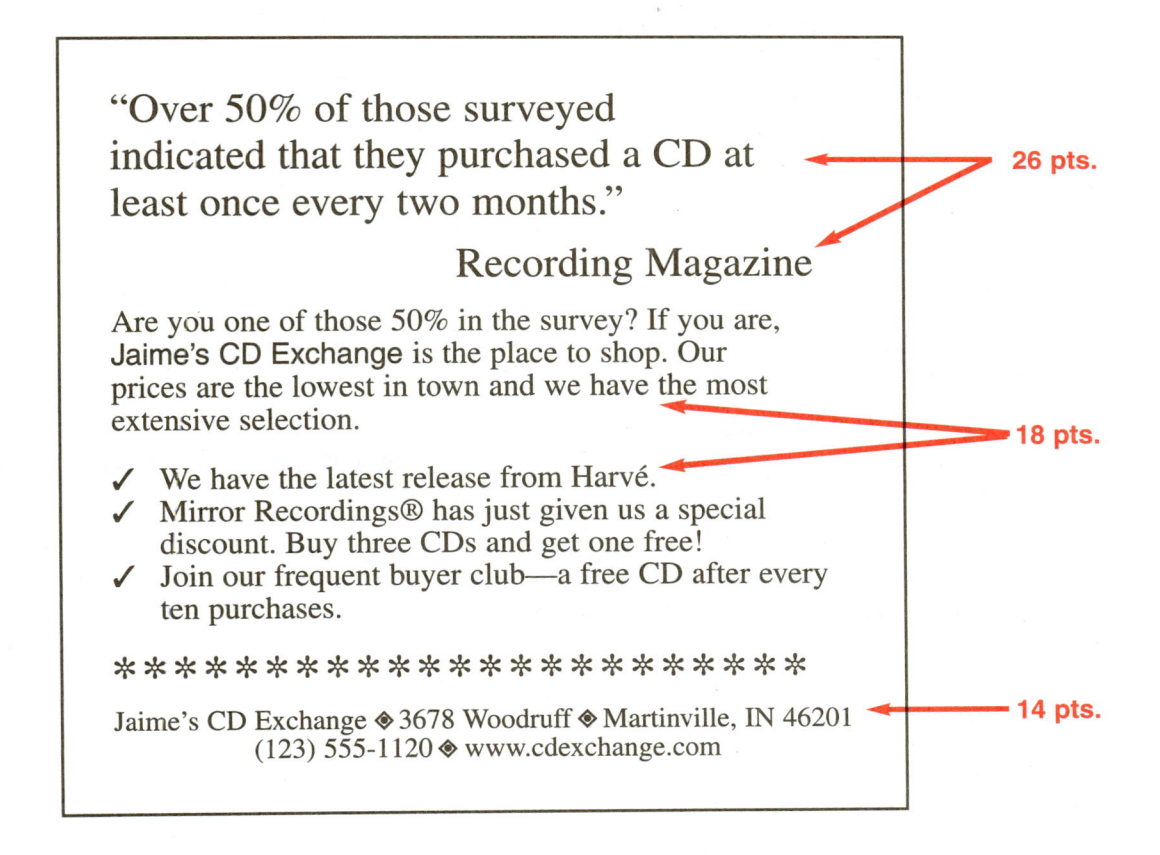

"Over 50% of those surveyed indicated that they purchased a CD at least once every two months." — 26 pts.

Recording Magazine

Are you one of those 50% in the survey? If you are, **Jaime's CD Exchange** is the place to shop. Our prices are the lowest in town and we have the most extensive selection. — 18 pts.

- ✓ We have the latest release from Harvé.
- ✓ Mirror Recordings® has just given us a special discount. Buy three CDs and get one free!
- ✓ Join our frequent buyer club—a free CD after every ten purchases.

✽✽✽✽✽✽✽✽✽✽✽✽✽✽✽✽✽✽✽✽✽✽✽

Jaime's CD Exchange ◆ 3678 Woodruff ◆ Martinville, IN 46201
(123) 555-1120 ◆ www.cdexchange.com — 14 pts.

5 Create Columns

Focus

- Create columns, set gutter widths, change page orientation, and insert column breaks.

Columns and Gutters

Pages can be arranged in single-column, two-column, or three-column formats. Generally, columns are of equal width; however, they can be formatted with different widths. The space between columns is called a *gutter*; generally this space is .5".

Before you use columns in a document, you must first determine the number of columns, the width of the columns, and the width of the gutter.

Remember these guidelines:

- Having too many columns on a page makes the lines of text too short to read with ease and tends to crowd the page.

- Use 10- to 12-point text for columns. Type smaller than 10 points is difficult to read; type larger than 12 points leaves too much space at the end of a line, giving the column an uneven, "snaky" appearance.

- Wide gutters lighten a page with white space, making the page easier to read.

Some word processing programs give you more control of these choices than others. With some programs, you may use your mouse to increase or decrease column width. Others provide a dialog box for choosing spacing requirements.

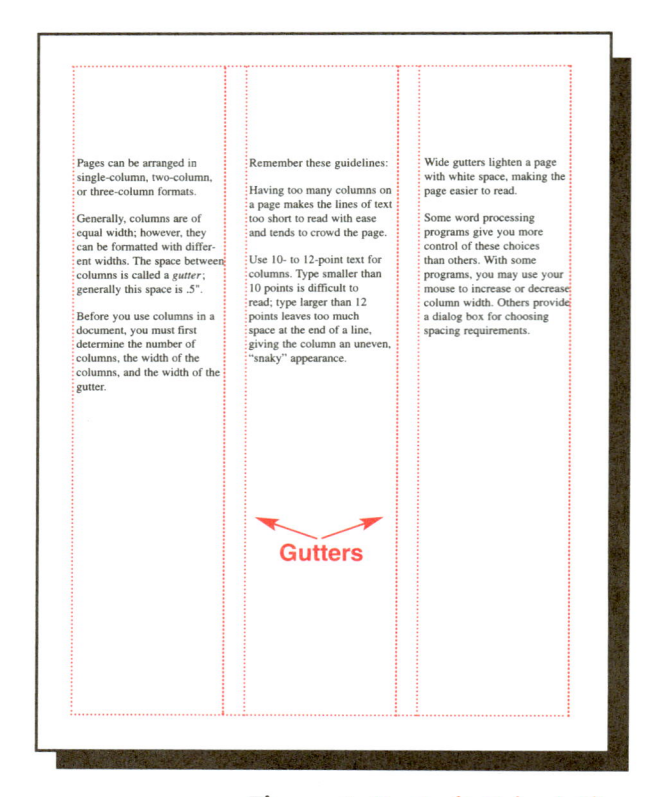

Figure 1 Portrait Orientation

Page Orientation

Documents may be printed in **portrait** (vertical) orientation or **landscape** (horizontal) orientation. Note the differences between Figures 1 and 2. Portrait orientation is the default, but it may be changed in any document.

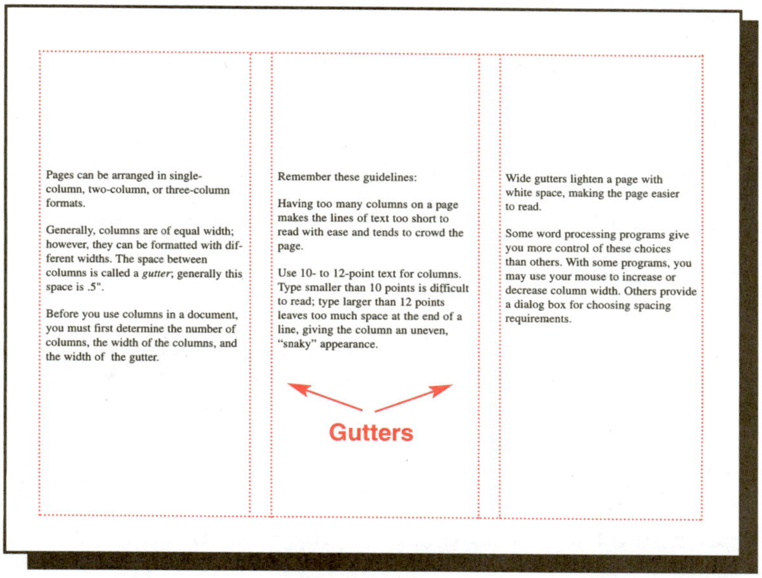

Column Breaks

When columns are set, text flows automatically from the bottom of one column to the top of the next column. If you wish to move to the top of the next column before you have filled the first column with text, you need to insert a column break. The cursor moves to the top of the next column, and you can begin your next block of text.

Figure 2 Landscape Orientation

Using My Software

Access Help for functions and record the steps for your software.

SOFTWARE FUNCTIONS	STEPS
Set number of columns.	
Change width of columns.	
Change width of gutters.	
Set page orientation.	
Insert column break.	

Create Columns

Activity 5-1: Set Columns and Column Breaks

1. In a new document, open the file **news**.
2. Set the margins to 1" on all four sides.
3. Change the text font to 12-point serif font.
4. Set 3 columns, using the default gutter of .5".
5. Insert a column break before the Shakespeare article.
6. Keep **news** open to use in Activity 5-2.

Activity 5-2: Change Orientation and Column Widths

1. Change the page orientation to landscape.
2. Change the columns to 2 (not equal-width columns).
3. Make the left column 2" wide (see illustration below).
4. Press Return or Enter after the Shakespeare and Around Town articles.
5. Save the document as **ACT5-2** and print it.

Arts Festival Date Set
The annual arts festival will be held on May 8 and 9 in the Civic Center.
Interested artists are encouraged to submit paintings, sculptures, crafts, drawings, ceramics, and other artwork.
There is no entry fee for high school and college students. Non-students must submit a $5 non-refundable fee for each entry by May 1.
Contact Janet Seymour at (976) 555-1230 for more information.

Shakespeare Play Declared Success
By Randall Smitherspoon
Saturday's presentation of "A Midsummer Night's Dream" at the high school was a delight to behold.
The adaptation of the Shakespearean play has won several festival contests and is scheduled to be performed again at the state contest.
Samantha Thomas was particularly appealing as Titania, but Lin Wan stole the show as Puck. The other members of the cast contributed as well to the overall professionalism of the production.
Ms. Sarah Whittington, who directed the play and is the theatre production teacher at the high school, deserves to be commended. The hours of work that went into the show were clearly apparent.

Around Town
The Community Drama Workshop will be holding auditions on May 1. Call John Harper at 555-2354 for more information.
Johnson Taylor will be giving a poetry reading on May 14 in the courthouse square.
Paula Patterson-Wright has had an article accepted for publication in the August issue of the Sentinel Gazette.

Summer Musical in the Park
This summer, the musical in the park will be a series of short pieces composed by members of the Butterfield Composition Society. These original pieces reveal a great deal of talent in our midst. Plan to come hear them.

Activity 5-3: Set Columns, Gutter Widths, and Column Breaks

1. In a new document, set the orientation to landscape and the margins to .5" on all four sides.

2. Set the columns to 3 with 1" gutters.

3. Using a large, appropriate font (48 points maximum), key and center the text shown in the first column.

4. Insert a column break to take you to the top of the middle column. Insert a second break to take you to the top of the third column.

5. Using an appropriate font (20 points maximum), key the text in the third column.

6. In the first column, insert the graphic **lion** from the template disk. Position, copy, paste, and resize the graphic as needed.

7. In the second column, insert the graphics **rabbit**, **lamb**, and **cow**. Again, resize, copy, and paste the graphics as needed. Use your judgment to decide what arrangement will make the most impact.

8. Save the page as **ACT5-3** and print it.

Lions and Tigers and Bears

Sorry,
there won't be any.

But there will be a petting zoo sponsored by the **Wildlife Rehabilitation Center**.

Sunday, April 18
2-5 p.m.

Admission:
$2.00 for adults
$1.00 for children under 15

Proceeds will be used to buy food for the center.

Improve the Look of Columns

Focus

■ Enhance the look of documents with columns by adding hyphenation, justifying columns, adding extra space between paragraphs, and creating banner headings.

Hyphenation

You can improve the look of columns, particularly narrow ones, by using your software's *hyphenation* option. By controlling how lines wrap, hyphenation creates a more even right edge to each column and reduces the distracting "rivers" of white space wandering between columns. Note the differences between the columns in Figure 1. The first column has not been hyphenated and has a distracting "snaky" appearance. The second has been hyphenated, giving it a more even right edge and more consistent white space.

Text Without and With Hyphenation

This column shows what happens when hyphenation is not activated in a document. Notice how much spacing there is at the end of some lines. This gives the column too much white space.

This column shows what happens when hyphenation is activated in a document. Notice how much less spacing there is at the end of some lines. This gives the column a better look.

Figure 1 Hyphenation

When hyphenation is turned on, words are divided automatically according to standard word-division rules. However, you should double-check the word division in your documents and change the word breaks as needed using your software's manual hyphenation option.

Your software may allow you to determine the consecutive number of lines that end with a hyphen. Generally, allow no more than two consecutive lines with hyphens. You also can determine how much space to allow at the end of a line before a hyphen is required. The smaller the space allowed at the end of the line, the more even the edge of your column will be.

Justification

Justification or alignment refers to the placement of text on a line. By default, text is left-aligned (starts at the left margin). Text may also be aligned at the right, centered, or justified (see Figure 2). Justified text is aligned at both the left and right edges of a column. Space is distributed between the words rather than at the end of each line.

Left-Aligned Text
This text has been set to align left. It is the most common alignment and one you will use most often. It is the default alignment which means that your word processing software will assign it automatically to all text when you open a new document.

Justified Text
This text has been both justified and hyphenated so that you can see that the words spread across the line more evenly. Newspapers and newsletters use justified text. It gives a sense of order and precision to a page.

Right-Aligned Text
This text is aligned to the right. It is not an alignment that is used often, although for display purposes it can be quite useful. Notice that you have right-aligned several of your previous activities in this book.

Figure 2 Justification

Improve the Look of Columns

Newspaper columns frequently are full-justified. Justified text gives a sense of order to a page. (But it can also close up white space that gives the page a sense of openness.)

Hyphenation improves the look of justified text because it reduces the amount of space that must be distributed within the lines. Avoid justifying lines if the text size is large.

Spacing Before and After Paragraphs

You can improve the look of a column by increasing the space before or after paragraphs. This option adds extra space between paragraphs, but not between lines of a paragraph. The extra spacing is measured by line spaces (single, 1.5, or double) or in points (one line is 12 points).

The space added before or after a paragraph is in addition to the spacing already set for the lines. If your line spacing is set to 1.5 and you add .5 space before or after a paragraph, you will now have a double space between paragraphs.

Banners

Banners are headings that span multiple columns (see Figure 1). To create a banner, key the text for the banner (in a single column) and then define the number of columns for the body text. Some word processing software requires a section break within the page in order to set two different column arrangements. Banner headings may be easier to prepare if you key the entire document, select (highlight) the text to place in multiple columns, and then make your column choices.

Using My Software

Access Help for functions and record the steps for your software.

SOFTWARE FUNCTIONS	STEPS
Turn on hyphenation.	
Justify text.	
Set spacing before and after paragraphs.	
Create banners.	

Activity 5-4: Create a Newsletter

1. Open **news** in your word processing program. Set margins on all sides to 1".

2. Key and right-align the following text for the newsletter title information (also called the masthead).

   Butterfield, Maine
   Arts and Letters
   April-May

3. Choose appropriate fonts and sizes for the masthead. ("Arts and Letters" is shown in 48-point type.)

4. Choose appropriate fonts and sizes for the body copy and headings. (The body text is shown in 12-point type.)

   Hint: In the illustration, only two font styles are used in the articles: one for the body copy and one for the article headings.

5. Left-align the headings and full-justify the body copy.

6. Turn on hyphenation.

7. Set the spacing after all paragraphs at .5 line spacing or 6 points.

   Hint: Select all the text below the masthead to change it all at once to the desired style, size, justification, and spacing. Then change the headings to another style, size, and alignment.

8. Set the masthead as a banner and set the articles to three columns.

   Hint: Once your columns are set, pressing Return or Enter at the end of the word "May" in the masthead will cause the three columns of text to move down.

9. Insert a column break after the Arts Festival article and another after the Shakespeare article. The extra white space will be used for graphics added in the next activity.

10. Press Return or Enter after the Around Town article to separate it from the Summer Musical article.

11. Save the newsletter as **ACT5-4**.

Activity 5-5: Enhance a Newsletter

1. Open **ACT5-4** if necessary.
2. Place a drop cap in the first paragraph of the Arts Festival article. Set it to drop two lines.
3. Cut the Summer Musical article and paste it below the Arts Festival article. Delete the last line, "Plan to come hear them."
4. Use bullet styles of your choosing to set off the list under the Around Town article.
5. Place a dingbat at the end of the Festival, Musical, and Shakespeare articles to show that the article is complete.
6. Place the graphics **note** and **masks** as shown below. Resize them and choose the no-wrap option.
7. Insert a line to separate the masthead from the body of the newsletter.
8. Save the newsletter as **ACT5-5** and print it.

6 Use Drawing Tools, Lines, and Borders

Focus

■ Apply lines and borders and use drawing tools to add shapes to your documents.

Basic Shapes and Lines

The drawing toolbar makes it easy to insert simple shapes, adding polish to documents. The basic shapes are rectangles, ovals, and lines (also called rules).

Within these three basic shapes, you can choose a variety of graphic treatments:

- Lines and borders may be wide, narrow, or invisible. They may be solid black, a shade of black, or a color.

- Lines can be dashed, thick, or thin and can have arrows on the ends.

- Shading can be added to fill in the background of a shape. This background "fill" may be a solid or a gradient (shade) of black, color, a pattern, a texture, or a picture. Use fill and shading subtly, so it doesn't overpower the page. Check also that text within the shape is still readable after applying a solid or gradient fill.

- Shadows and 3-D effects add depth and sophistication to graphics by allowing you to change the direction of lighting, the reflection on the surface, or the angle. The 3-D and shadow options are available in recent software versions.

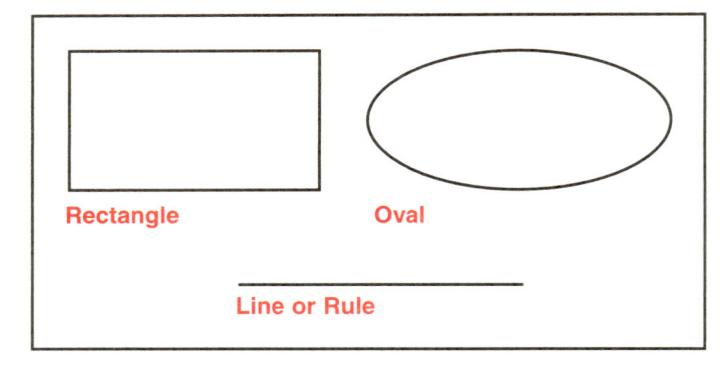

Figure 1 Basic Shapes

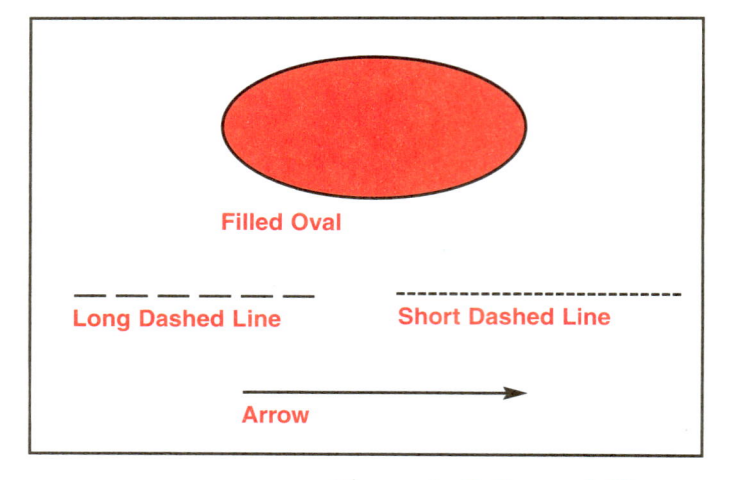

Figure 2 Enhanced Shapes

Manipulate Shapes

To move a drawing object or shape, select it and drag it to a new location. A shape can be sized just like a graphic, by using the mouse to pull on the shape's handles. A shape can be combined with other shapes, rotated, or moved in front of or behind another shape. The same grouping/ungrouping action used for editing vector graphics is used for editing shapes.

Special Shapes

Depending on the word processing application, the drawing toolbar may include other shape tools such as a polyline (a line with one or more angles), polygon, or arc. These shapes are used to "draw" irregularly shaped objects such as a triangle with unusual angles or a curved line.

To create a polygon or a polyline, select the tool, click and drag, and then click each time you want to change an angle. When you have finished drawing the polygon or line, double-click to stop drawing.

Recent versions of word processing software feature preformatted shapes. These shapes can be added to existing clipart graphics.

These shapes may include stars, special arrows, flowchart icons, banners, and callouts. *Callouts* contain a block of text and connect it to a graphic, similar to the "balloons" used for dialog in comics. Earlier versions of software require adding a text box to the callout figure.

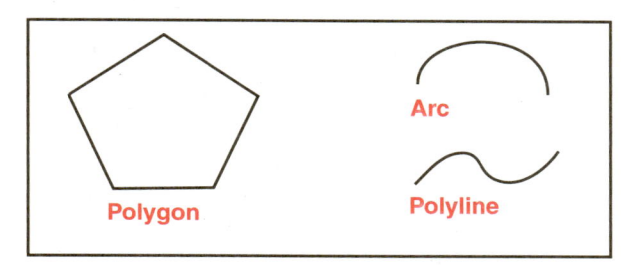

Figure 3   Basic Shape Tools

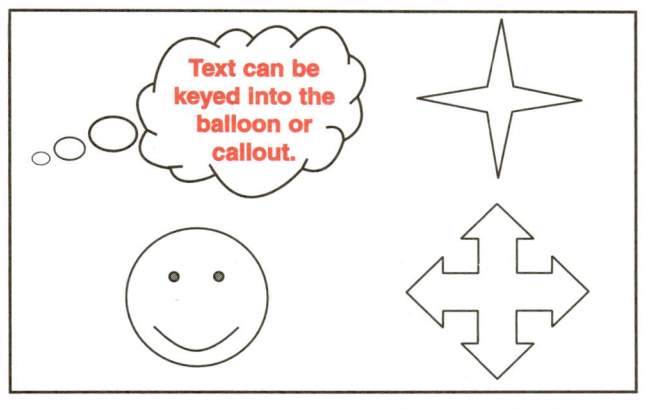

Figure 4   Preformatted Shapes

Graphic Tips

Holding down the Shift key while drawing a line will force the line to remain straight. Holding down the Shift key while drawing an oval will create a perfect circle. Holding down the Shift key while drawing a rectangle will create a square. Holding down the Shift key while resizing a graphic will usually change the size of the graphic, but maintain the proportions.

Text Box

The *text box* tool allows you to add text to a drawing or shape. Without the text box, it is not possible to add text within an illustration. Text boxes are used also to set off special blocks of text from the rest of the page. To use a text box, insert a box with the tool and then key the text in the box; tables and charts can also be inserted into a text box.

> A text box like this does not have to adhere to the standard column format of the rest of the page. You can place it wherever you want.

Text keyed within a text box can be formatted just like any other text (bold, italic, fonts, etc.). You can also add a fill to the background of the text box; move the text box by selecting it and dragging it to a new location; and rotate it.

In the example at the right, a text box was added to an oval and formatted with a texture. Text within the text box was formatted in Arial bold. The text box is set to "no line" and "no fill," making it appear to be part of the oval. The shape and the text box can be grouped and repositioned as a unit.

Super Saturday

Page and Text Borders

Borders are another effective means for setting off or displaying words, paragraphs, or the entire page. When you add a text box or insert an object, its shape is automatically defined by a thin line or border. Borders can be formatted by changing the thickness, color, or pattern. You can choose to use a border on any or all four sides of the box.

> Your word processing software may give you the option to shade one or more words, which will give the text emphasis. Or you may want to shade an entire paragraph.

← **Paragraph with Border and 10% Shade**

A graphic page border similar to Figure 5 on page 49 may be one of your choices. While graphic borders can add impact to a page, care should be taken to avoid

> You can place borders around all four sides of a paragraph or page, or you may be able to choose the number of sides that will have a border.

← **Top and Bottom Paragraph Border**

using a border that will overpower the page. A border similar to Figure 6 that flows down the left side and across the bottom of the page can be used as an independent graphic and incorporated into the page design. A design such as Figure 6 might be used for an invitation or poster.

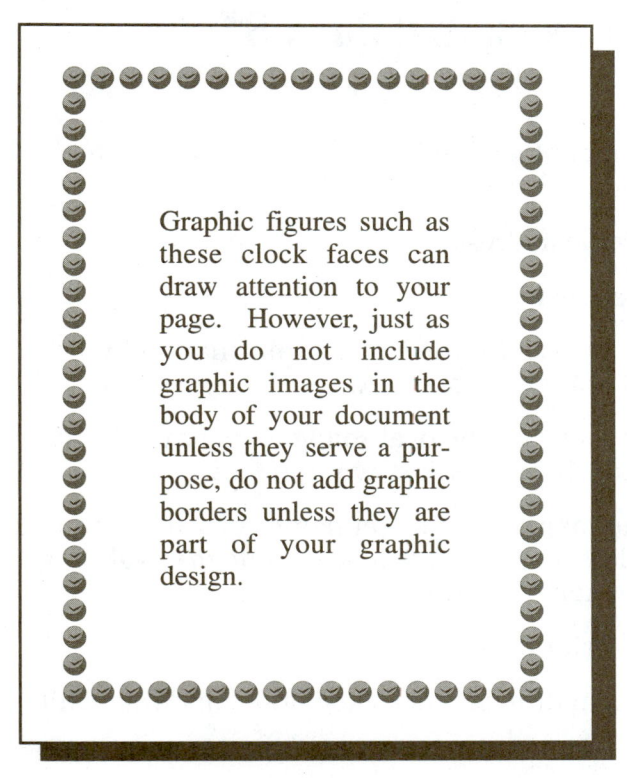

> Graphic figures such as these clock faces can draw attention to your page. However, just as you do not include graphic images in the body of your document unless they serve a purpose, do not add graphic borders unless they are part of your graphic design.

> Use a border such as this for a casual invitation.
>
> You would not use it in a business document.

Figure 5

Figure 6

Using My Software

Access Help for functions and record the steps for your software.

SOFTWARE FUNCTIONS	STEPS
Open drawing tools.	
Access shapes.	
Access wrapping.	
Access shade/fill.	
Create paragraph borders.	
Create page borders.	

Use Drawing Tools, Lines, and Borders

Activity 6-1: Use Basic Shapes, Text Boxes, and Page Border

1. Set all margins at 1.25".

2. Examine the flyer on page 51. Center the main heading in a 26-point font. Key the address and bulleted list in a 20-point font.

3. Draw two lines, one above and one below the address.

4. Center the title and right-align the bulleted text.

5. Create a text box for the contest information. Center the contest information in the same font as the bulleted text. Shade and border the text box.

6. Create the lines of the map using the line tool. Use the oval shape to mark the location of Butterfly Ranch, or create a simple butterfly by drawing two triangles.

7. Insert and position text boxes for the street names. Key street names in a 10-point font; choose "no line" to hide the text box borders. Position a text box inside the oval shape; key "Butterfly Ranch"; choose "no line" to hide the text box borders.

8. Place a border around the page. Save and print the flyer.

    Note that the address and the contest information balance each other, and that white space balances the map.

Activity 6-2: Use Preformatted Shapes (For Word 97 or WordPerfect 8 or later versions)

1. Open a blank document and key information for the fax cover page shown at right.

2. Explore the preformatted shapes available to you in your software.

3. Use an arrow similar to the illustration to draw attention to the error information.

4. Save and print the fax cover sheet.

Activity 6-3: On Your Own

1. Create a notepad for use in your school or office.

2. Design a logo using the drawing tools.

3. Save and print the notepad.

Date:
To:
From: Albert Garza
Number of Pages (including this cover):
Message:

⇨ Call (654) 555-1300 if there is an error in transmission.

THE BUTTERFLY RANCH
GRAND OPENING
March 18, 9 a.m. — 6 p.m.

3467 Wallcreek Road
Abilene, Kansas

- ◆ Hundreds of Butterfly Items Available
- ◆ Perfect Gift Items for Every Occasion
- ◆ Conveniently Located
- ◆ Major Credit Cards Accepted

Register to Win a Diamond Butterfly Pendant!

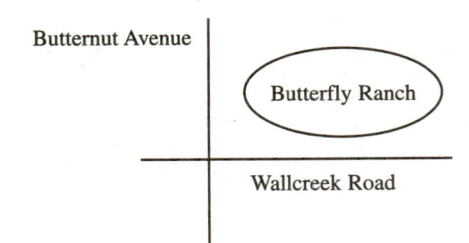

Butternut Avenue

Butterfly Ranch

Wallcreek Road

7 Create and Apply Styles

Focus

- Use styles to format documents efficiently.

Styles

Styles allow you to format similar types of text consistently. Three examples of styles applied on this page of your book are the lesson title, the side headings, and the body copy. Each style consists of a specific font type, size, color, attribute, and line spacing. Applying these styles to the same types of text throughout the book gives the entire book a consistent, professional appearance.

Word and *WordPerfect* contain many built-in styles that you may apply as you format documents. Each style has its own unique font, size, and attribute. You can change these styles or create your own styles. In this lesson, you will apply the built-in styles and you will modify these styles and create your own.

Built-In Styles

Generally, any standard formatting element can be part of a style. You can access built-in styles by clicking the Styles option under Format on the menu bar (Figure 1) or by selecting a style from a drop-down menu on the toolbar (Figure 2). To apply a built-in style, select the text to which you wish to apply the style. Then choose the style you wish to apply. A description of the style lists the specific formatting elements of the style. Built-in styles are named for the purpose for which they are designed.

Should you change a formatting element of a style, all text set in that style is updated automatically and consistently.

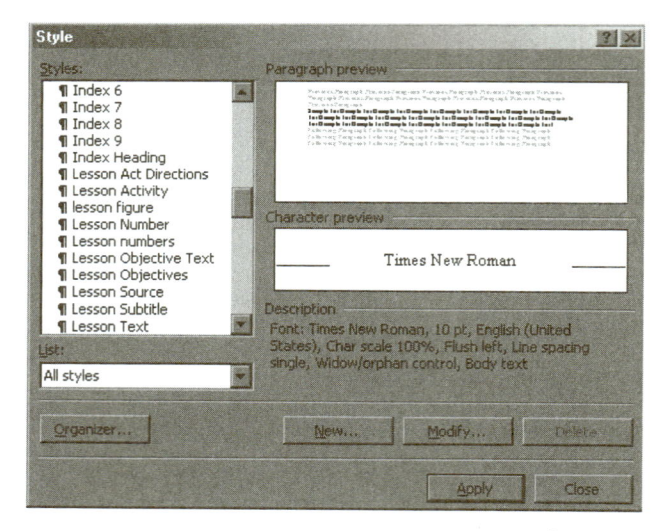

Figure 1

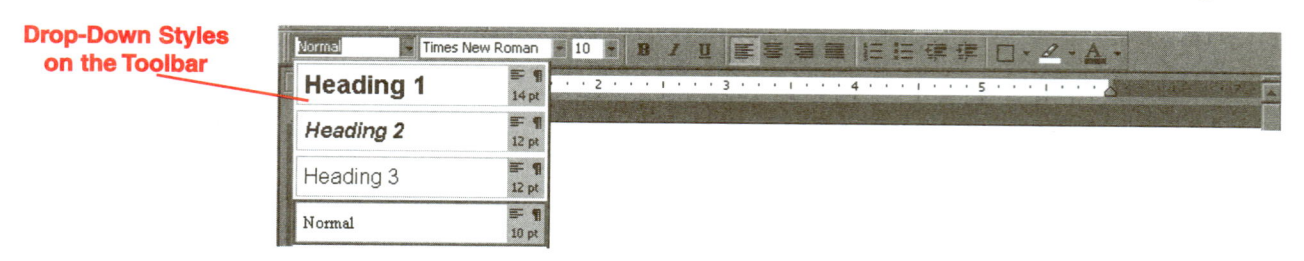

Drop-Down Styles on the Toolbar

Figure 2

52 Create and Apply Styles

Formatting elements that can define a style include the following:

- bullets
- font type, size, color, and attributes
- hyphenation
- keep lines together
- line spacing
- numbers
- paragraph borders
- paragraph alignment
- paragraph indention
- paragraph margins
- shading
- space before and after a paragraph
- tabs and leaders
- widow/orphan control

Creating Styles

Styles can be created for characters or paragraphs. To apply character styles, you must select the text and then apply the style. Paragraph styles consist of a number of character styles that are stored under one style name.

An easy way to create a new paragraph style is to base the new style on an existing one. In *Microsoft Word*, format the paragraph as you want it, click on the Styles box, and type over the existing style name with a new name. *WordPerfect's* easy-to-use dialog box allows you to define each formatting element of the style. You should give each style a unique name that indicates its purpose.

Once the style is in place, other styles can be based upon it and modified as needed. The new style is given another name to indicate its purpose.

Editing a Style

The advantage of using styles is apparent when you want to change the format of your text. For example, assume that instead of formatting separately each side heading within a document, you applied a style to all side headings. Later, to change the format of the side headings, you simply edit the style for side headings rather than reformat the individual headings. Edit styles by choosing Styles from the Format menu. Select the style you want to edit from the list (if necessary, click *Modify*). Change the attributes.

Using My Software

Access Help for functions and record the steps for your software.

SOFTWARE FUNCTIONS	STEPS
Apply styles.	
Create styles.	
Edit styles.	

Create and Apply Styles

Activity 7-1: Apply Styles

1. Open **News** from the template disk.

2. Click on the first heading. Open the Styles dialog box and locate a style appropriate for a headline, or use the Styles drop-down menu on your toolbar. Apply the style.

3. Click on each heading and apply that same style.

4. Click on the first body paragraph. Locate and apply an appropriate style from the Styles dialog box. Click on each paragraph and apply that same style.

5. Return to the Styles box and modify the styles you used for headings and body. Change the size and the spacing before and after a paragraph. Apply these styles. Notice how quickly the changes were made.

6. Save the document and print it.

   Your printout may be different from the illustration at right.

Activity 7-2: Create and Apply Styles

1. In a new document, open the Styles dialog box. Notice that letter styles such as closings may already be available to you. You may rename and modify these or create your own styles using the following names and formatting elements.

   S&S letter—distinctive font, 12-point with no hyphenation
   S&S date/closing—based upon S&S letter, indent 3" from left margin
   S&S body—based upon S&S letter, double space(2 lines or 12 points) after paragraph

2. Key the letter shown, applying each style to the designated text. Space between letter parts as indicated.

3. Create a letterhead similar to the one shown.

4. Save the letter as **ACT7-2** and print it.*

---

* From this point on you will save and print all of your work, unless directed otherwise.

Create and Apply Styles

Stuff and Stuff
Office Supplies for Tomorrow
366 Broadmoor Drive
Wichita, KS 67221-2326

S&S date/closing → July 14, ---- (Quadruple-space—QS)

S&S letter → Harriet S. Lafferty
Deloit Enterprises
9834 Heartland
Omaha, NB 68107-5550 (Double-space—DS)

S&S letter → Dear Ms. Lafferty: DS

S&S letter → Thank you for your interest in our bulk paper clip purchasing program. We have found through the years that companies such as yours can benefit from our program, which includes recycling up to 450 pounds of used paper clips every year. I am enclosing a brochure that features this program as well as others that may be of interest to you.

One of our representatives will contact you next week to discuss your order and to answer any questions. We look forward to serving you. DS

Sincerely QS

S&S date/closing → Harrison L. Johnson
Senior Paper Clip Distributor DS

S&S letter → Enclosure

Activity 7-3: Create Styles

1. Open **contest** from the template disk or key the text from the model on p. 57 as unformatted text with no columns.

2. Set all margins to 1". Turn on hyphenation.

3. Open the Styles dialog box. Create a style called "contest" making the font 12-point Times New Roman (or a similar serif font). Set the alignment to full justified and spacing after paragraph to 1.5 line or 6 points.

Create and Apply Styles

4. Create a style called "contest rules." Base it on the "contest" style (so font and size are already selected) but change the style so the second line indents approximately .2" (hanging indent).

5. Create a style called "contest headings." Base it on "contest" but change the font attribute to bold, and change the paragraph spacing *before* the heading to 1.5 lines or 12 points.

6. Create a new style called "contest title." Choose a sans serif font, 16-point bold. Set it to center with 2 lines or 12 points after the paragraph.

7. Create a final style called "contest information." Base it upon "contest," but place a border around the paragraph and shade it 10%.

8. Highlight the entire page or use Select All. Choose the style "contest," which will change the entire page to the font and size you have chosen.

9. Select the title and choose the style "contest title."

10. Change the text below the title to three columns. You may want to review the lesson on creating columns.

11. Select the heading "Purpose" and choose the style "contest heading." Do the same for "Guidelines," "Judging," "Copyright Laws," and "Entry Requirements."

12. Insert a column break before "Judging" and before "Copyright Laws."

13. Select the numbered entry requirements and set the style to "contest rules."

14. Select the entry fee and entry deadline and set the style to "contest information."

15. Add a graphic at the beginning of the text to balance the page. It should span two columns, similar to the illustration.

16. Place a border around the page.

Activity 7-4: On Your Own

1. Create two sets of styles for use in your school or business. You may modify styles already in place or create your own. One set of styles will be for use in memos; another will be used in letters.

2. Create a list of specifications for each style that includes:

   - font type, size, and attributes
   - alignment
   - line spacing
   - spacing before and after paragraphs

3. Save and print the list of specifications.

Desktop Publishing Contest

Purpose

The goal of the Desktop Publishing Contest is to expand the use of desktop publishing in classrooms.

Guidelines

This contest is open to all public and private school students in grades kindergarten through twelfth grade, with judging in the appropriate level of competition.

All documents are to be solely the work of the submitting student(s) and must be verified on the entry form.

Students may use any available software.

The content or theme may be any appropriate subject.

The categories are brochure/pamphlet, newsletter, business document, flyer, poster, or advertisement.

Judging

The criteria will be graphic appeal, creativity, and content.

The judges for this contest will come from the professional arena with experience in desktop publishing.

Projects will be given one of the following ratings: superior, excellent, good, or fair. Projects receiving a superior rating will be judged a second time to establish overall winners in each category within each competition level.

Contest results and certificates will be mailed to all participants.

Copyright Laws

All copyright laws are to be followed. Violations will result in disqualification. All graphics, photos, clip-art, etc. that are not student-made shall be cited on the project description form.

Entry Requirements

Each student will submit the following:

1. A hard copy on 8.5" x 11" paper.
2. A copy on disk (either standard 1.44 or larger) of the completed project.
3. A completed project description form.
4. A completed release form.
5. A completed entry form for each entry.
6. A check for $5 per entry.

Multiple entries from the same school may be mailed together and a single check may be enclosed. However, separate forms must be provided for each entry.

Entry fee: $5 per entry.

Entry deadline: All entries must be postmarked no later than March 15.

8 Present Numerical Information with Charts

Focus

- To create/insert charts in your documents.

Charts and Graphs

Charts help readers visualize data by showing the relationships between numbers. Using charts as visual tools to deliver information gives you two advantages:

1. Readers grasp visual information more quickly than verbal information.

2. Graphic elements help keep your reader's attention. A chart will usually be the focus of a page.

Charts fall into three basic categories: pie, bar, and line, as shown.

Line graphs may be used to show numerical change over time, such as the change in the price of a stock over a period of days, weeks, or months.

Bar charts are useful for visually comparing amounts. A bar chart might be used to compare the sales figures among members of a sales force.

A pie chart shows the relative size of different subcategories of a single item. A pie chart could show what percentage of your income is used for clothing, housing, food, and recreation.

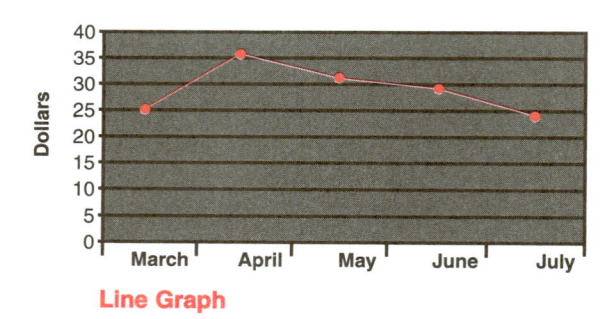

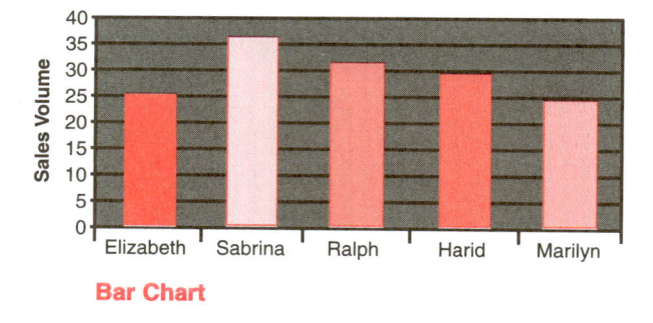

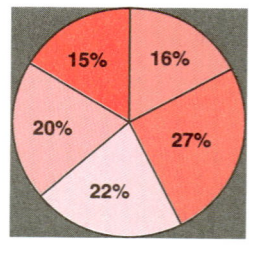

Figure 1

58 Present Numerical Information with Charts

Charts have the following six elements in common:

X-axis—horizontal axis used for categories

Y-axis—vertical axis used for values

Labels—x- and y-axis column headings or segment headings

Title—general description of the information

Legend—colored key that defines the numerical data used in the chart

Data series—the numbers entered into the datasheet from which the chart is created

Menu options are available to add titles, labels, and legends. These options also allow you to choose the color or pattern for the lines, bars, or pie segments and the background. Generally, you will need to double-click on the chart for the menu options to appear. Double-clicking on any part of the chart will also call up formatting options for that part of the chart.

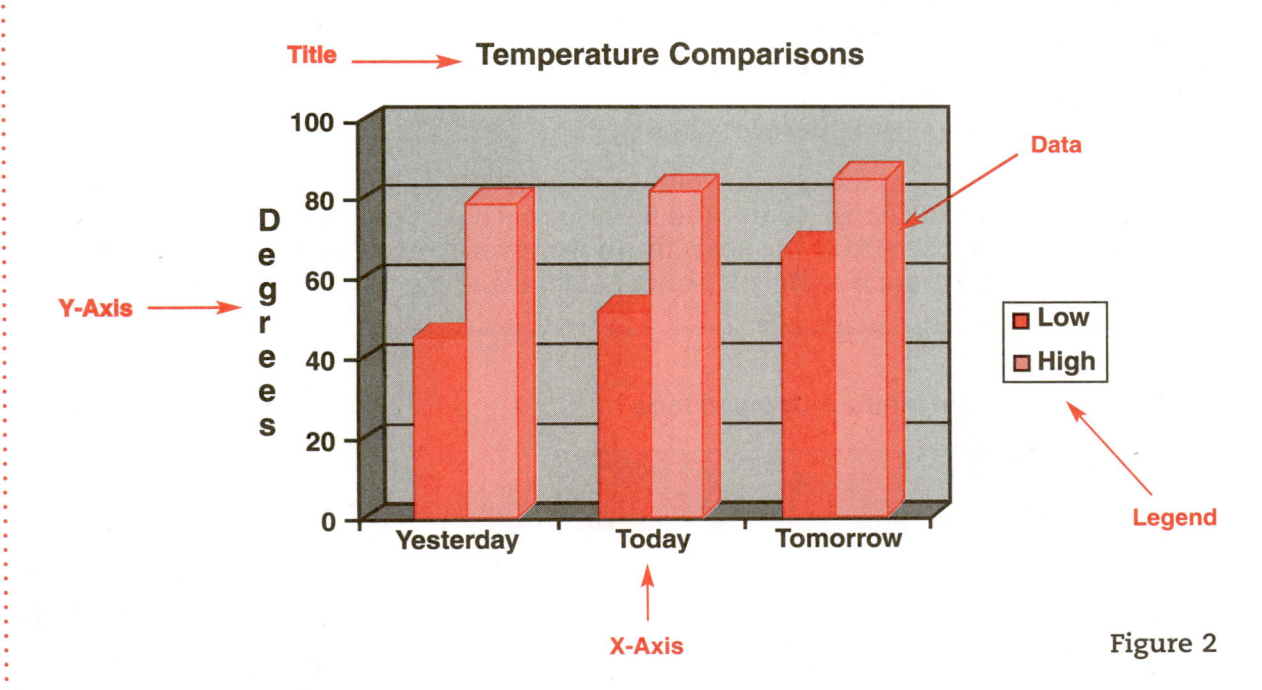

Figure 2

Graphic Tip

A table is a columnar list of information. A chart is the graphic representation of that information using bar, line, or pie graphs.

Present Numerical Information with Charts

59

8

Create Charts

Some software has a Chart option or button as part of the menu or graphics toolbar. In other software, such as some versions of *Microsoft Word*, you select the menu option Insert, choose Object, and then select Create New. A list of programs appears from which you can choose a charting or graphing program (see Figure 3).

Once you have selected the appropriate method to create a chart, a table "shell" or datasheet will appear for you to key in your information (see Figure 4). You should first delete unnecessary sample information already in the table.

Your program converts the data in the datasheet to a chart format. You can choose to see the chart in bar, pie, or line graph format using chart formatting buttons on your toolbar. Click outside the datasheet to remove it, leaving only the chart visible. Double-click on the chart to make the datasheet reappear.

As you change or add to the data in your datasheet, the chart will reflect the new information. You can choose colors and fonts for each part of the chart using menu options. Changing the size of the chart by dragging one corner affects many of the features of the chart, such as the placement of labels.

Figure 3

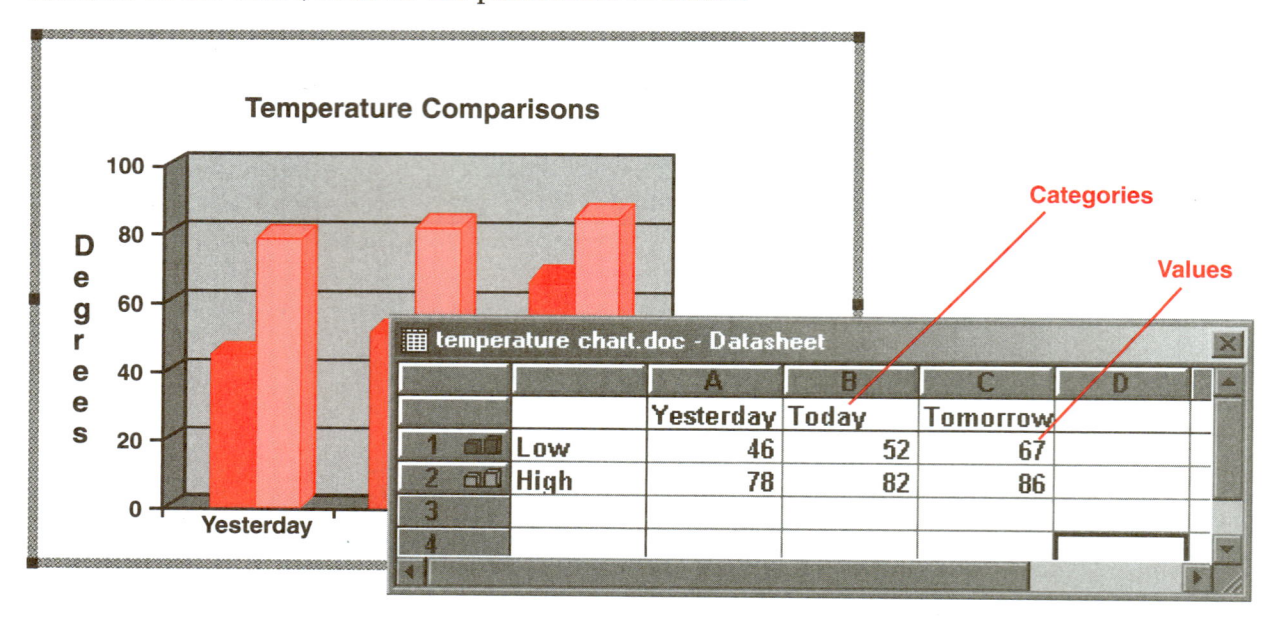

Figure 4

Present Numerical Information with Charts

Insert a Chart from a Spreadsheet File

Like graphic images such as clipart, charts created in a spreadsheet program may be inserted into a word processing document. To insert a chart created in another program, choose the menu option Insert an Object (under Insert) and then select Create from File. Figure 5 shows the dialog boxes that appear in recent versions of *WordPerfect* and *Microsoft Word*.

Once you have inserted a table or chart that was created in another program, you are limited to only a few standard graphic options, such as adding borders and shading, moving, and resizing. You do not have the extensive formatting options that are available when you create a chart within your word processing software.

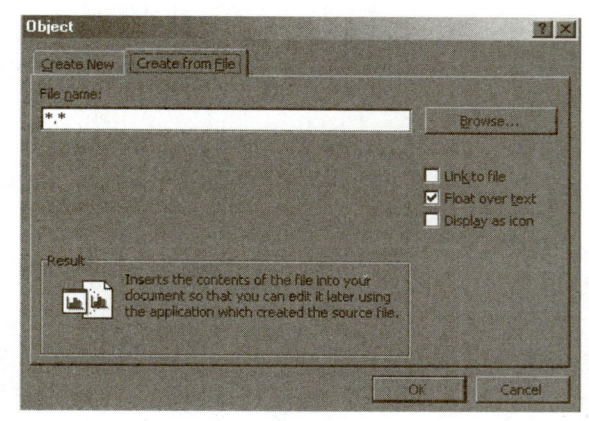

Word

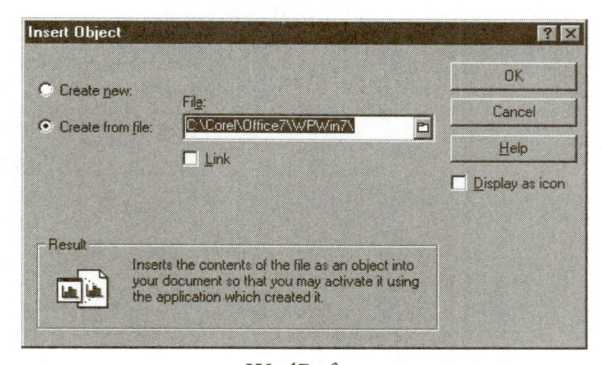

WordPerfect

Figure 5

Graphic Tip

In *Microsoft Word*, the "Float over text" check box found on the Insert dialog box gives you two choices. When it is checked, the chart (and other graphics) can be moved wherever you want. When it is not checked, the chart is placed in the text at the insertion point. Once it is in place, you cannot move the chart, but you can align it just as you would text.

Using My Software

Access Help for functions and record the steps for your software.

SOFTWARE FUNCTIONS	STEPS
Create charts.	
Format charts.	
Insert charts.	

Present Numerical Information with Charts

Activity 8-1: Create a Chart

1. In a new document, create a new chart.

2. Key the temperature information into the datasheet as shown.

3. Experiment with the different chart types and then choose the bar chart (columns or cluster subtype shown below).

4. Experiment with different colors for the bars.

5. Add a title and y-axis label similar to the illustration. (The values, or numbers, shown on the y-axis appear automatically.) Experiment with different font sizes and placement for the categories, titles, and legend.

6. Enlarge the chart so the X-axis labels appear in horizontal format. Experiment by changing the size of the chart.

	Yesterday	Today	Tomorrow
Low	46	52	67
High	78	82	86

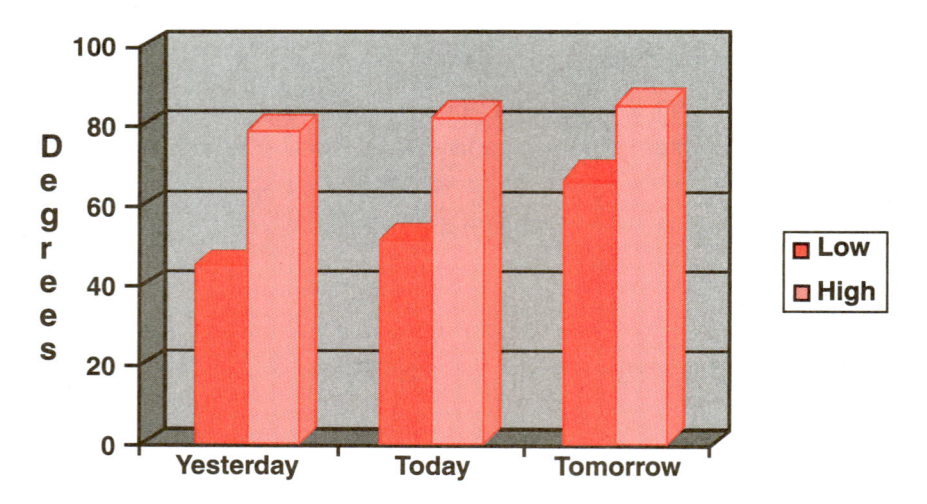

Temperature Comparisons

Present Numerical Information with Charts

Activity 8-2: Create a Chart

1. In a new document, set all margins to 1.5" and choose landscape orientation.

2. Key the flyer text as shown, using a large font (36 points maximum) for the top section and a smaller font (24 points maximum) for the bottom section. Right-align the top section and left-align the bottom section.

3. Create a chart. Key the following information into the datasheet/table as shown (in five columns and two rows):

Working	Sleeping	Eating	Recreation	Unknown
8.6	7.4	2.8	2.4	2.8

4. Choose the option for a pie chart. Experiment with the color and font options available. Choose the option to show percentages for the data series.

5. Set the chart to wrap and the chart size to 5". Choose appropriate border and shading.

6. Place a decorative border around the page.

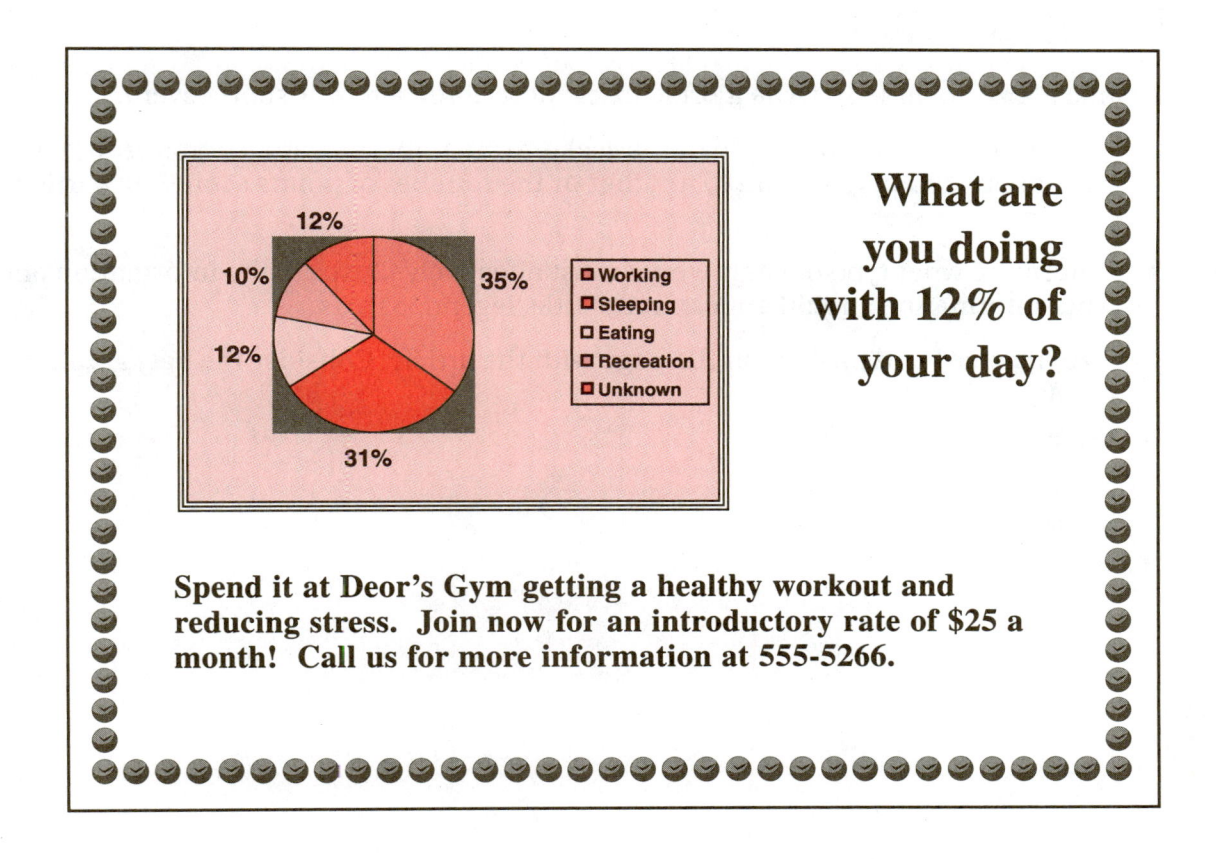

What are you doing with 12% of your day?

Spend it at Deor's Gym getting a healthy workout and reducing stress. Join now for an introductory rate of $25 a month! Call us for more information at 555-5266.

Activity 8-3: Insert a Chart

1. In a new document, set 1" margins and a tab at 1".
2. Center "Memo" in a 48-point sans serif font.
3. Key the memo (shown on page 65) in a 12-point serif font.
4. Tab after "To," "From," "Date," and "Subject" to align the information.
5. Insert the chart **sales** from the template disk, using the Insert Object/Create from File option.
6. Make the chart approximately 5" wide, maintaining proportions.
7. Place the chart at the bottom right corner of the page.
8. Notice that design elements are positioned so the white space at the lower left balances the space at the upper right. The sales chart provides the primary focus of the page, with the text providing secondary focus.

Activity 8-4: On Your Own

1. In a blank document, write a brief article describing a recent sports event.
2. Create a chart to illustrate the numerical information, such as a comparison of the win/loss record of one team to another or the number of points scored by particular players.
3. Determine what type of chart would most effectively illustrate the information and what information should appear in the title, legend, or axis.
4. Size the chart and place it on the page with the article. Consider the best graphic placement.

Memo

To: Book Haven Managers

From: Joanna Grimes
Sales and Promotion Manager

Date: February 13, ----

Subject: Summer Sales Figures

We observed an interesting phenomenon last year while tracking our spring sales figures. In the past, we have anticipated an increase in early summer book sales, but we have not seen a similar increase in magazine sales. Last year, however, magazine sales increased faster than book sales for April and May.

To take advantage of this shift in purchasing decisions, we would like you to reposition your magazine display space beginning in April by placing it in a position to catch the shopper's eye. We believe that you will see additional revenue in May as a result of this change.

Film sales did not increase as much as expected. You will be receiving promotional film brochures next week to use in your stores.

Let's all pitch in and work on building those sales that we know are ours.

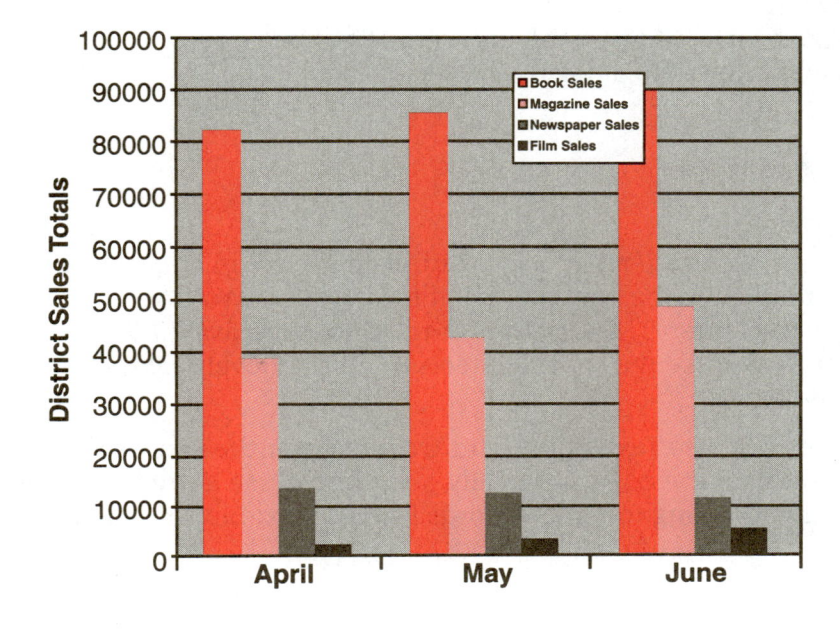

9 Add Special Effects

Focus

- Use special effects such as watermarks and TextArt/WordArt.

Watermarks

Watermarks are subtle text or graphics applied to the background of a page. Watermarks are reduced in intensity or "faded" to appear to be nearly a shadow on the page. They may provide information about the nature of the document (such as indicating draft versions or confidentiality). Watermarks are also used as decorative backgrounds or for company symbols, logos, and slogans on business correspondence.

Successful watermarks emphasize the content of the document without interfering with a document's readability. Watermarks add valuable information and visual interest to a page.

Here is an example of a watermark. Notice that it is lighter than the other text and that text is designed to appear on top of it.

Figure 1

Words as Artwork

TextArt in *WordPerfect* and WordArt in *Microsoft Word* are additional special effects that enhance the appearance of text. TextArt/WordArt treats words as a graphic design element. Many formatting options are available. Care must be taken, however, not to overuse the special effects or let the novelty of the feature spoil the document's good design.

When you use TextArt or WordArt, you enter the text in a special text box rather than directly on the page. Generally, you should use a single word or a short phrase to avoid crowding too many words into the text box and making the result unreadable.

Once your text is entered as artwork, you can make a variety of choices about its appearance. You can change the font, size, attributes, and spacing. If you stretch or shrink the text box after you have chosen a font size, the font size will increase or decrease automatically to fit. You also can curve, stretch, and rotate your words and apply graphic treatments such as shadows, colors, or outlines. Below are a few examples of words used as artwork.

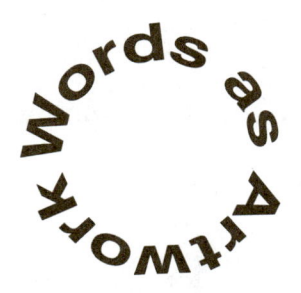

Figure 2

Using My Software
Access Help for functions and record the steps for your software.

SOFTWARE FUNCTIONS	STEPS
Add watermarks.	
Insert TextArt or WordArt.	

Add Special Effects

Activity 9-1: Add Watermarks

1. Set 1" margins and landscape orientation; key the invitation.
2. Change font to a 36-point sans serif style. Reduce the size of the listed items to 20 points. Bold **"Graduation Party"** and the date and time.
3. Choose an attractive graphic bullet for the listed items.
4. Place a graphic border around the page.
5. Insert the template file **grad** as a watermark. Enlarge the graphic to fill the page.

You are cordially invited
to Rick and Amy's
Graduation Party

☞ **Bring your enthusiastic good wishes.**
☞ **Bring your own chairs.**
☞ **Bring something to share.**

May 15
7:30 p.m.
Call 555-1414
for directions to the party.

Add Special Effects

Activity 9-2: Use Words as Artwork

1. In a new document, create "Thirty Ways" with TextArt/WordArt, using any appropriate design selection.

2. Select font style, attributes, and size. Set alignment. Select bright colors for the outline and the inside color of your text. Deselect the text box by clicking outside it.

3. Insert the heart as a shape or from clip-art/scrapbook. Then add a text box within the heart and key the text as shown.

4. Place a border around the page.

5. Move the TextArt/WordArt text box around the page. Rotate it. Change the size of the box. How do these changes affect the appearance of the page?

6. After printing, consider your design choice for the title text. Would the title page create an interest in the paper to follow? Did the TextArt/WordArt enhance the appearance of the page?

Activity 9-3: On Your Own

1. Design the first page of a newsletter to be used as a template for future newsletters.

2. Use TextArt/WordArt to create the title of the newsletter. Choose the vertical option and place the title so it runs "down" one side of the page.

3. Include spaces for the date, the volume, and the issue of the newsletter.

4. Create a set of styles for the article titles, the article body, and other recurring features.

5. Build in places for graphic images to be inserted.

6. Consider whether a watermark would be appropriate.

7. Save **ACT9-3** as a template file. (The extension will be different than a document file.)

10 Create a Portfolio

Focus

- Create a portfolio of business documents to demonstrate your desktop publishing skills.

Portfolio for WindMill Farms

WindMill Farms has been in business for years, but wishes to update its image as it expands into new markets. You will design a series of desktop-published materials, including a business card, trade ad, letterhead, fax cover sheet, memo form, and newsletter.

To increase WindMill Farms' name and logo recognition, use the same font for the company name and the same company logo throughout these documents.

Activity 10-1: Create a Business Card

1. A business card measures approximately 3" x 2" with 1/4" margins. You will create the card on a full sheet, but set the margins comparable to the size of a business card: left margin 2.75", right margin 2.75", top margin 4", bottom margin 5.5".

2. Center the text. Insert a rule above the e-mail address. Insert the template file *windmill* as a watermark.

3. Place a 3" x 2" rectangle around the text to see what the card will look like when printed.

WindMill Farms
Madeline Savoy Harrison, CEO
3578 Briarhaven
Mayfair, GA 31207
912.555.2334

MSH@windmillfarms.com

Activity 10-2: Create an Ad

1. Create a 4" wide ad for display in a trade publication. Set the left margin at 2" and the right at 3".

2. Set a tab at 2" for the company information. Key the text shown at the right. The web address may turn into a hyperlink. That will not affect your ad. (Choosing Undo from the Edit menu will remove the hyperlink in *Word*.)

3. Insert the windmill graphic three times, reducing as necessary. Set the graphics to No Wrap. Place a rule beneath them.

4. Notice that the windmill is no longer used as a watermark. Now the windmills graphically balance the company information. The rule helps maintain a sense of consistency and creates a box effect around the windmills.

5. Where does your eye focus first? How are the design elements arranged in the ad? Who is the audience?

Activity 10-3: Create a Drawing

1. WindMill Farms has used the same windmill graphic for years as part of its advertising identity. Experiment with a new windmill graphic to help update WindMill Farms' image.

2. Use the line drawing tools to create a new drawing to serve as a rough guide for a professional graphic artist.

3. Try out the new windmill drawing by placing it in the business card or ad.

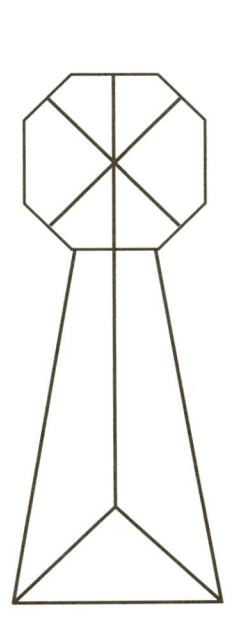

Create a Portfolio

71

Activity 10-4: Create a Letterhead Template

1. Create a letterhead for WindMill Farms using the information from Activities 10-1 and 10-2. Save the file as a template rather than as a document file so that it can be reused each time a letter is created.

2. Create two styles: one for the date and closing lines, and one for the body of the letter.

3. Save the letterhead as **ACT10-4** with the template extension.

Activity 10-5: Format a Business Letter

1. Using the letterhead template **ACT10-4**, key the letter shown on page 73.

2. Apply the letter styles you created in Activity 10-4.

Activity 10-6: Create a Fax Cover Sheet and a Memo Form

1. Create a fax cover sheet, again using **ACT10-4**.

2. Insert a text box for the fax transmission error information.

3. Save the fax cover sheet as **ACT10-6a**.

4. Modify the fax cover sheet to create a memo form. Remove the fax information and add memo headings (To:, From:, Date:, Subject:). Save as **ACT10-6b**.

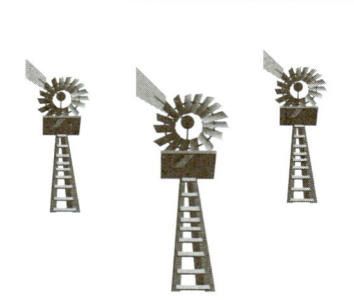

WindMill Farms
Madeline Savoy Harrison, CEO
3578 Briarhaven
Mayfair, GA 31207
912.555.2334

MSH@windmillfarms.com

If an error occurs in transmission, please call 912.555.2335

FAX

To: **From:**

Date: **Number of Pages** (including this one):

Message:

WindMill Farms
Madeline Savoy Harrison, CEO

3578 Briarhaven
Mayfair, GA 31207
912.555.2334

MSH@windmillfarms.com

July 14, ----

John Rosson, Vice President
City Bank and Commerce
9211 Boston Ave.
Mayfair, GA 31226

Dear Mr. Rosson:

Thank you for your interest in WindMill Farms. As you know, we have expanded our market in order to offer a much broader selection of merchandise than in the past. We have been delighted with the response of our customers to this new venture. We anticipate our growth to be in excess of fifteen percent this year alone, with new orders coming in rapidly for next year's holiday sales.

As we discussed last Tuesday, additional funding will be necessary in order for us to realize fully the potential of these new opportunities. City Bank and Commerce has always been very helpful in providing such resources, and we look forward to continuing this relationship.

I am enclosing a brochure showing our new lines as you requested. If I can be of any more help, please feel free to contact me.

                              Sincerely,

                              Madeline Savoy Harrison, CEO

Enclosure

Activity 10-7: Create a Newsletter

1. Set up a page with two columns and 1" margins on all sides. Create styles for the body and headings; key the newsletter.

2. Justify the body and apply hyphenation.

3. Use TextArt/WordArt for the newsletter title.

4. Select graphics from the Internet or your clipart selection. Crop them as needed.

5. Use a drop cap to begin each article and a symbol to close each article.

6. Create a line chart from the table below to show the growth of calico sales. Add labels and a title.

7. Add a border to the page.

8. Position a text box at the bottom of the page for the company information.

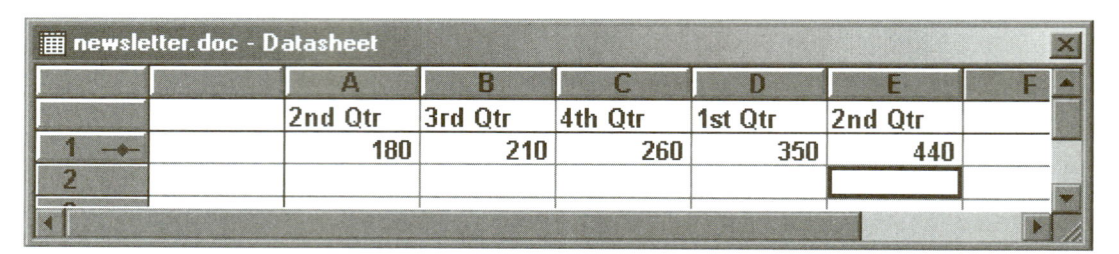

newsletter.doc - Datasheet						
	A	B	C	D	E	F
	2nd Qtr	3rd Qtr	4th Qtr	1st Qtr	2nd Qtr	
1	180	210	260	350	440	
2						

Activity 10-8: Create a Title Page

1. Create a title page for your portfolio. Include your name, the name of the class, the time your class meets *or* the period, your school, and the date.

2. Use appropriate graphics, fonts, and designs to enhance the look of the page.

3. Bind your portfolio documents together with the title page as the first page.

WindMill Farms

July 1999

WindMill Farms is proud to announce the expansion of its lines to include calico skirts, wall hangings, and quilts. Calico has become the surprise seller of the year at regional and state craft fairs, and we do not believe interest in this fabric has peaked. Sales figures shown below (provided by Fabrics Unlimited) confirm our belief.

Our calico selection includes the traditional muted tones as well as brighter, more modern colors. One of our most popular colors has been tangerine fuzz, which combines both ecru and a splashing orange. Skirts are offered in both the broomstick and the newer crisp style.

Our wall hangings are created from the finest calico with the images woven into the fabric rather than painted on. This makes them perfect for children's rooms as they are fully washable. The tiger and lamb series now includes ten new designs in six sizes.

Quilts have always been spectacular sales builders, drawing in crowds wherever they are displayed. Calico quilts are sturdy, washable, and light. They are crafted to become heirlooms, but they are still affordable. Order five quilts and we will ship them at no charge.

Sundials have become essential for every landscaped yard. Our sundials are made of brass and stainless steel, guaranteeing years of durability. They have been featured in *Today's Homes* and were awarded the Designer "Best of Show" at last year's fair. Craft fair goers will love both the look and feel of these exquisite pieces of workmanship.

Order one today and watch it go out the door tomorrow.

Johnathan Sanders is back. After an absence of several months, Johnathan has returned to the craft market with four new designs for quilt hangers.

His hangers have always had a place of honor in our catalog, and these new designs promise to be even better. They are constructed from hand-cut oak that has been rubbed to a fine finish. They come in six shades ranging from light to dark; perfect for every décor.

Paired with our calico quilts, these hangers can make this year to exceed all sales expectations.

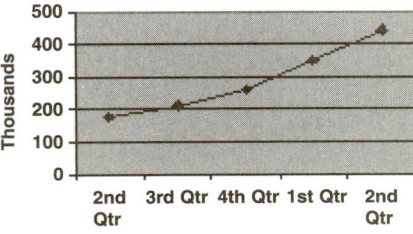

Calico Sales for 1998-99

Quarter	Thousands
2nd Qtr	~175
3rd Qtr	~225
4th Qtr	~260
1st Qtr	~350
2nd Qtr	~450

3578 Briarhaven • Mayfair, GA 31207 • 912.555.2334 • www.windmillfarms.com

Appendix: Glossary and File Formats

Asymmetry—unbalanced arrangement of elements on a page, creating an interesting sense of novelty

Attributes—typographical features including bold, italic, underlined, small caps, shadows, or color

Bitmap—a graphic file format utilizing pixels to create a map of an image

Callout—a block of text, sometimes enclosed within a shape, that is connected to a graphic image

Clipart—graphic images that may be accessed through a word processing program, bought on CD-ROM, or downloaded from the Internet

Dingbat—a graphic symbol selected from a set of symbols available in most word processors. Sometimes gathered in a font selection called *Wingdings*

Flow—the visual path created by arrangement of elements within a page's design

Focus point—the visual element in a page's design that the viewer notices first

Group—to create a single graphic image out of several graphic segments so you may modify the graphic as a unit

Gutter—the white "river" of space between columns of text

Pixels—the tiny squares that make up a bitmapped image

Styles—a word processing tool for applying formats to different types of text quickly and consistently

Symmetry—balanced arrangement of visual elements in a page's design

Text box—a tool for adding text to a graphic or for setting off special text on a page

Typography—the arrangement and appearance of type on a page

Ungroup—to revert a graphic image to a series of graphic segments

Vector—a graphic file format utilizing mathematically determined segments to create an image

Watermarks—subtle text or graphics applied to the background of a page

White space—a blank area on a page designed to provide a visual break and to give other elements greater impact

Z pattern—a visual path that starts at the upper left of the page, moves to the upper right, then down to the lower left, and finally to the lower right

BITMAP FILE FORMATS	
Extension	Format and Image Type
.bmp	Bitmap
.clp	Windows Clipboard
.cut	Dr. Halo
.dib	OS2
.eps	Encapsulated Postscript
.gif	Graphic Interchange Format
.iff	Amiga Electronic Arts
.img	GEM Paint
.jpg or .jpeg	Joint Photographic Expert Group
.lbm	Deluxe Paint
.mac	MacPaint
.msp	Microsoft Paint
.pbm	Portable
.pcd	Kodak PhotoCD
.pcx	Paintbrush
.pgm	Portable Graymap
.pic	Pictor
.png	Portable Network Graphics
.ppm	Portable Pixel Map
.psd	Photoshop
.ras	Sun Raster Images
.raw	Unencoded Pixel Data

BITMAP FILE FORMATS (continued)	
Extension	Format and Image Type
.rle	Windows
.tga	Targa
.tif or .tiff	Tagged Image File Format

VECTOR FILE FORMATS	
Extension	Format and Image Type
.cdr	Corel Draw
.cgm	Computer Graphics Metafile
.drw	Micrografx Designer Draw
.dxf	Autodesk
.emf	Enhanced Metafile
.gem	Ventura
.hgl	Hewlett-Packard Graphics Language
.pct	Macintosh Draw
.pdw	HiJaak Draw
.pic	Lotus Development
.sdw	Word Pro Draw
.wmf	Windows Metafile
.wpg	Word Perfect